from the Grave

ISBN: 145632196X
ISBN-13: 9781456321963

LCCN 2010916404

from the Grave:

A Story of Life, Even in Death

Tyler Rambeau

Cover images by: Erin Keenan

Contents

Preface

This is a book of love and hurt, hope and courage and victory, and what others might see as defeat. This is a book that preaches the same convictions that my mother had in creationism, but it also holds sensitivity to those with varying beliefs—I even think the latter persons might hold more to gain. This is a book that acknowledges that pain is painful regardless of the source, but with a greater focus on pain from the devastation of death. Most notably, this is an ode to a life worth sharing in an intimate openness with others who might be going through their own issues, and need to know they are not alone.

There is no manual or handbook that could ever lead each individual in his need to be led out of darkness. If someone did presume to have all of the answers, I'd consider him to be a bit too arrogant for my taste. Nonetheless, I do aim to aid the healing process by examining the lessons I continue to learn from my mother's life that have brought me back to a place of comfort.

As humans, we are just smart enough to run ourselves stupid in circles searching for answers to impossible questions. When our desire for answers isn't met, we look for someone to blame: doctors, other family members, and even God. Instead, we need to start searching for peace, realizing that we will never have answers to the wrong questions. Rather than, "Why me?" or "Why does this happen to good people?" or "Why so young?" we should be asking, "What can I gain from the examples of an amazing person who did more with less?" Taking responsibility for this mind-set not only glorifies the lives of those we love, but also rises above the suffering of bereavement.

Lastly, this story could have been told in a multitude of ways, and by many people that were touched by my mother's graceful existence. With the blessing of my family, I am taking on this daunting endeavor in an attempt to convey to the masses the magnitude of her impact, so her life lives on.

Note: some names have been changed and all quoted scriptures are from the New Living Translation.

Introduction

In the early morning hours of August 6, 2009, a superhero was lost. The news did not make headlines, no spandex suits were retired, and crime did not suddenly run rampant again. Aside from traditional forms of comic star recognition, she put up a heroic fight against the injustices of doubt, defeat, and fear; all without the flamboyancy of a cape or signifying symbol. In fact, she blended in perfectly with average people like you and I, but beneath the exterior, there was something extraordinary in her being. She stood boldly at five foot three, and drove the largest SUV the market had to offer, not to announce the size of her carbon footprint, but to ensure safety for the precious cargo she was constantly carrying. Her name is Anna Rambeau, she is my mother, and her kryptonite was cancer.

Her message was amazing, her certainty of survival was unwavering, and I can't count how many times I heard her say to me in a valiant tone, "Tyler, it's going to take a miracle for me to survive, but I will have my miracle, you know why?

Because God can't use me from the grave!" This is the message I am responding back to her now:

Dear Momma,

Many days I can't find the motivation to get out of bed in the morning, but I never seem to sleep at night. I write this in hope that someone who is praying will read it or knows another who is going where you are, and can personally deliver my message to you in the event that God cannot hear us over the combination of cries.

Where my once confident life has lost certain purpose with your loss, the certainty of your efforts is still there to full-fill my fath when I feel abandoned by the desperate need for the tangibilty of your irreplaceable embrace.

Your fight did not fail my father, my brother, or sisters, or me. Your life was one of relentless perseverance and impact; a legacy that will forever live on. Your constant reassurances of recovery to us, that the testimony of a divine victory could not be shared from the grave, were not defeated in death or disease, for you are not in the ground, but alive in heaven, and I am still here to continue what you started. It seems you overlooked one thing. You were diligent to your work on earth. You raised a grateful and loving son; a writer and a storyteller, and I will tell your story...

Chapter 1

The Birth of a Superhero

My mother was born on October 27, 1964 in Victoria, Texas, to Al and Olivia Plummer. She was the last of four children. At a considerably young age she showed signs of the acutely goal-oriented adult she would grow up to be. Toward the end of a family meeting—my mother's exact age lost in generational scrolls of translation, but said to be less than five years old—all of the kids were asked what they wanted to be when they grew up. As the assortment of answers rolled down the line toward her, she was asked, "Anna, what do you want to be when you grow up?" She affirmatively responded, saying, "I just want to be old enough to say sh*t and not get a spanking for it."

She came from a family of storytellers, every member of which was undeniably unique. Loud, eccentric, and ready to pop the corks on all of the wine bottles, they were the crowd you wanted to be around for ceremonious events. It was clear that she got her distinctive, charismatic laugh from the roar of my grandfather, Papa Al, who would demonstrate it after each story he would tell. It was nothing short of hilarious to hear her two sisters, Aunts Junie and Chris, chime in with their own blaring sounds. And of course there was their brother. Every family has one; the crazy uncle that is wildly inappropriate in every occasion, who makes you cringe around children and adults alike in anticipation of the punch line of each joke (or virtually anything he might say), but you can't ever seem to get enough, either.

Anna, however, was born with a sincere innocence unmatched by those that helped shape her own lovability. I like to intertwine multiple recountings of her childhood memories into one of my favorite anecdotes of hers. I picture a hand-sewn summer sundress on a cute adolescent version of my mother that I never knew outside of sepia tone pictures. I see her with her bangs (cut with the help of her best friend) that would cause any parent both aggravation and adoration all in the same moment over the lost locks. In this story, she is accompanied by her loyal dog Shep. (Anna rescued Shep, hiding him in her backyard playhouse, and keeping him alive on peanut butter amidst an unbearable summer heat.) She is strolling down a dirt road in a small Texas town, happily picking fresh bluebonnets. Upon her eager arrival home to share her pretty findings, her own mother, who boasted a sarcastic sense of humor beyond a child's comprehension, informs her of the state law against picking these flowers. Her mother says that she could go to jail for this. As ironic fate would have it, there was a knock at the door shortly after; it was a police officer. *"Noooo!!! "* she screams, slamming the door in his face crying her eyes out in disbelief that her seemingly angelic afternoon would have her taken from her home and thrown in jail for a floral felony. She runs straight to the bathroom, locks and barricades the door, and refuses to come out even after it turned out to simply be the recovery of her brother's stolen bike.

Despite the pleasantness of most of her early recollections, the rest of her young life was anything but. I don't believe there was ever a time in her life that she was able to know her own mother in healthy form. As her mother endured a battle with cancer for the better part of ten years, Anna was raised with the intricacies of disease being a daily commonality. Those with similar experiences, however, can testify that the overwhelming amount of loving support encircling affected families is more than enough to rival feelings of despair or suffering. One would think that the length of time would have been an emotional and physical drain (and this notion definitely has a level of accuracy), but Papa Al has never failed in his consistency to tell me that he enjoyed the opportunity to be his wife's strength and her comfort in her time of need. He's said that he would have done so without limitations. It's amazing which perspective people will dwell on though.

In his elder years, my Papa Al is constantly smiling and kind; a merry man that looks like Santa Clause without a beard, but round, jolly, and containing a boisterous presence that can quickly fill any room. Like many grandparents, he always comes bearing gifts, usually in monetary form (no more than ten to twenty dollars, but always something other than a typical bill). He's handed my siblings and I labeled sacks of one hundred dimes, rolls of forty quarters, and ten Sacagawea gold-dollar coins when they first came out. He is quirky, funny, and memorable. He represents the head of that side of my family's traceable bloodline, and is also our oral historian. There isn't a time when he has failed to include each individual detail about exact locations, dates, and first and last names of whomever happened to cross his path.

An underlying backwoods good ol' boy lingo is prevalent in his simile- and metaphor-filled explanations of others: "Wooo boy, he was as mad as a rattlesnake," "hotter than a dog in heat." His presentation made even the most serious tales amusing. You would think by now I'd be able to mimic him word for word, but I've rarely heard him tell the same story twice, unless otherwise requested for something specific. The archive of his mind is a spiraling rotunda, constantly unraveling new shelves in his library you've never known before.

Sometimes though, he speaks of his one and only wife Olivia. A subtle love lights up in his eyes, dusting itself off from its hiding place in the back of his chronicles. He tells of times when they were young and courting, when they were newlyweds in college at the University of Texas, the way Austin used to be, and later when he had to take care of her. There is a faraway, disengaged stare into a distant nothingness, affirming he is sharing something special deep within. He is still able to relive these past moments, if he can maintain his focus. Once he looks up to see if you are still listening, the shift happens. He says that through it all he only had one regret. I know this to be true, because although he genuinely believes that he's offering new information, they are the only words I have ever heard repeated.

Apparently one evening Olivia was having problems breathing through her oxygen machine. Knowing he'd had a long day, and that it would take a trip to the hospital to refill the bottle with air in the middle of the night, she tried not to be a burden to him while he was sleeping. The first attempted rustle was shrugged off. The problematic airflow persisted, and so did her efforts to rouse him, until he finally snapped back, agreeing to go in aggravation. The distant stare returns to his eyes as he speaks of her timid apology to him for not being able to breathe. I believe she was quick to understand the circumstances of someone who waited on her constantly and was slow to get offended by his unintended outburst. I believe she appreciatively slept easy the rest of the evening, and that he was sufficiently punished in the lonely car ride with the impulses of humanity and the awareness of an awoken conscience sitting next to him during the drive home. She forgave him by the time the sun rose, and I wish he could forgive himself in the same way, rather than living for many moons with the weight of a single regret.

Olivia finally succumbed peacefully at the age of forty-five. My mother was only thirteen. By that time, the rest of her siblings were already out of the house, taking on the world in their own respective ways. Papa Al had long before taken over the family business—running a funeral parlor. To diminish the eerie morbidity of this career, I would offer simply viewing it as a business (or in a lighter sense, by imagining my grandfather played by Dan Aykroyd and my mom as Anna Chlumsky's timeless character in the movie *My Girl*—ironically not having to change first names). But for Papa Al, this time business had become personal, and it hit too close to home. In life we try to never think of the unknowns of death, and we don't know how to get acquainted with the reality of its introduction when we are inevitably forced to meet it. Cancer is not discriminatory and has yet to reveal a cure. There is no immunity to the repercussions of its destruction, nor is there preferential treatment for anyone. Papa Al grew up in a different era; born during the Great Depression, and before shows like *Oprah.* In his world there was no widespread acceptance of showing emotions, especially for men of the time. Unable to adequately deal with the onslaught of his feelings, he left my mother alone for days, and sometimes weeks or more at a time on multiple occasions.

Oh how tender we have become in this generation, but not Anna. Oh no, not her, not back then, not ever. She told me the bread was always moldy and the milk always lumpy, and how she would spread peanut butter on tortillas, eat beans from the can, or learned to like cereal with water, rather than get dismayed by spoiled milk. You know the response you get from older people any time they hear a youthful complaint about the hardships of their times? You know, "Well when I was a kid we didn't have _____! We had to walk____ (insert distances and atrocious obstacles here)." Well, Anna and her family really did live atop of that hill, and she really did have to walk for miles to get to school (though there was no trudging through snowstorms for her in our southern state). Regardless, how many thirteen–year-olds do you know today that could accept these rigors as a natural lifestyle and later discuss them without a sense of depravation? She made such hardships seem like the common order, a coming-of-age normality. I would try to interject and give credence to her difficulties, but she never accepted the patronizing, or showed any deep-seated affliction. Most notably, there was never any judgment in her voice toward anyone for having it easier. She took pride only in the amount of love and security she was able to offer her own children, and how she could shelter them from any discomforts.

Chapter 2

Leaving Loneliness

Anna's solitude at home did not last long, but it would soon return. She moved in with her best friend, Sandra, and a wonderful family, the Kilgores (or Momma and Daddy K as everyone called them). Daddy K was a doctor supporting a large, loud family with the help of Momma K. She was a silly and whimsical woman that could easily be referred to as ditzy, but she had a far greater depth of love than the term suggests. She could be more aptly described as having a keen ability to laugh at her own amiable idiosyncrasies while maintaining the purity of a child's heart. One night when Momma K was taking the girls to a concert, Daddy K sarcastically said, "Be careful not to get stoned." Momma K looked back, sheepish for having forgotten something she might need to watch out for as a chaperone and said, "You know you're right. They just might throw rocks in the crowd."

From as far back as I can recall, Momma K was full of an energy that incited creativity each moment you were with her. We would eat popsicles, and then, using some old arts and crafts book she had, build a birdhouse with the sticks or devise our own "mad scientist" project. Even as I write this I am seeing a striking correlation between how memorable a person is with the amount of laughter in his life and the joy that accompanies each thought of him. On that note, you should have heard Anna and Sandra together. It's amazing to think sounds can be contagious: sneezing, one crying baby in a once peaceful room of many, and laughter. It was impossible to be anywhere near those two and not get sucked into the howling hilarity of their merriment, which typically ended in submission to a splitting pain in your stomach and someone saying, "Ooohhh, what in the world were we laughing at again!?"

I could never fathom my mother's fondness for those times in her childhood after her mother's passing, and her complete disregard for the unbearable pain that she must have experienced. She would always think about it for a second before quickly shrugging it off. She would say she didn't know how to explain it, but because she was encased by God's grace and an indescribable bubble of His that constantly surrounded her, she just didn't dwell on those feelings. I don't think my images of a "quarantine bubble" quite do this incommunicable divinity justice. I picture sweet little Anna walking with God's arms wrapped around her in the most comforting hug ever given. I think He hugged her through the warmth of family and the Kilgores. I think that where there was loss, she allowed the right people, who were always waiting, to enter her life and fill her voids instead of shutting everyone out. I think we all need a bit of God's love, in the form of those like Momma K, in our lives after a tough day.

During her freshman year of high school, one of Anna's classmates had a crush on a guy; a senior and charming bad-boy type. Needing flirtatious assistance, Anna was asked to standby while he told stories of his wild weekends partying, and the trouble he and his friends got into; something they knew nothing about yet. Anna was young and beautiful. He was fun and personable. Unfortunately, most girls in the same position are so naïve that they never have a fighting chance against those circumstances until it is too late. For Anna, it was.

The initial headfirst dive into the party world is exciting and seemingly forever festive. Once accepted, the crowd is inviting and inclusive. They shout your name and raise their glasses when you walk in the door. Before you leave, they wrap their arm around you, pull you in, and slur, "You're my best friend ever!" They love to talk about how funny and cool you are when you make a fool of yourself, but the nights are short-lived, and the mornings are agonizingly sobering upon the reality of many terrible decisions. The stories the next day quickly turn into hurtful rumors. You begin to question how someone could claim to be your best friend when they never remember anything from the evening. The charming bad boy loses his charm, but retains his badness; a product of the selfish existence that never finds fulfillment in substances.

He continually broke her heart, but she was already in too deep; trapped by the deceptive powerlessness of a premature first love. He moved from their small town to the city lights and lawless nights of Austin's party scene. Anna remained faithful. At the start of her senior year, Papa Al got a job in Austin. She was forced to move also, and she endured a lonely finish in a new school exponentially larger than the one that she was accustomed to. She was reluctant to make friends or plans while waiting for him to call on the weekends, but she was left waiting too many times. For the most part, he had his own agenda. He was to be my father.

Anna became pregnant at the age of twenty, and was left with no choice but to drop out of college. She was having a baby out of wedlock and without the consistency of a loyal boyfriend; a practice which wasn't nearly as prevalent, nor as socially accepted, as it is today. The majority of the time all she had was me, and I wasn't even born yet.

I was brought into the world with no shortage of love on a Saturday, the tenth of May in 1986; the afternoon before Mother's Day. She said I was her ultimate gift that she was eternally grateful for. It wasn't easy, but we made it work together. Correction: she made it work. While we had the help of friends and family, we survived due to her fight and her resilience; eventually living in the house at the daycare where she worked.

At that time, having gone from Anna to her new, more appropriate, title of "Mommy," she was searching for a higher strength and for forgiveness for the mistakes of her past (which, she said, ultimately led to the blessing that was me). She said I had helped save her life, and she wanted to devote her rebirth to her ultimate savior, the Lord, in church because of what she felt was a second chance at a righteous life. I was her little guy, and I sat by her side, but there was someone else who had an eye on her.

From across the auditorium, a man asked his buddy who that pretty lady was up in the front. The friend answered, "Her? Her name is Anna." The man then asked, "Oh, well who's that next to her?" His friend replied with, "That's her son, Tyler." "Wow," the man said. "I know! Yeah, we're actually going out." The last comment relating to them supposedly dating, didn't bother the man, who viewed her without judgment and who didn't perceive me as a burden or baggage. Considering he was hardly twenty-three, had recently finished earning his master's degree, and had just started a new job in a prominent bank downtown, it's hard to believe that he wished to pursue a woman with a child. It wasn't until later that his friend's comment about their relationship struck him as odd, "If they were some kind of couple, why weren't they sitting together?" The man suspected this was wishful thinking on his friend's end and decided to ask her out on a date for himself when the man soon stopped attending the church. His name was John.

The pastor of the church had told my mom he had heard in prayer that soon she would meet her future husband there. He had no clue who it would be, but assured her she would know him when she saw him. The first sighting happened on Easter Sunday in the spring of '88, when my mother's family was in town. He introduced himself to her, and when they asked who he was, she casually said it was the guy she was going to marry. They inquired for details about the man, but she knew no other specifics, and quickly realized her comment sounded a little silly. She took some friendly pokes from them on the matter after claiming a man she had never before met was the man she was going to marry.

Anna and John had both been attending a singles small group where they were able to get to know each other a little better. It was a Wednesday night service when John finally mustered up the nerve to ask for a date. They had been singing the hymn "Hosanna in the Highest," and as they were filing out afterward, he sang to her in the parking lot (with me shouldered on her arm) in the same tune, "Oh Anna, Oh Anna, will you go out with me?" Blushing, he later admitted that he was not wise in the ways of dating and might have been able to come up with a less embarrassing approach had he not been so nervous in the moment. But Anna found it endearing, and she agreed.

Shortly after, we were all set for the big date. That's right, we. We went to the movies, a Disney film, and she sat me between them in the theater. John bought snacks and a large bag of popcorn for all of us. I had an abnormal appetite as a child, and my mom confirmed that I willingly ate vegetables but didn't particularly care for sweets. She said the most I would ever ask for in the form of sugary products was a Pop-Tart, or a Cookie Monster cake she would bake for me on special occasions. But I did love popcorn, and still do to this day. The story goes that with barely any help I proceeded to demolish the entire bag before the previews were over. John looked at my mother in shock—first, for assurance that a two-year-old needing a car seat to see the movie could do such damage on a bag of popcorn, and second, for help as to what to do when I casually started tapping the empty bag against his shoulder for more (while never averting my attention whatsoever from the film). He says he got a look from her that said, "C'mon buddy boy. Are you willing to support us or what? Here's your shot to prove yourself. What are you gonna do?" In that instant he knew the best idea was to go get more popcorn.

Their infatuation and trust for one another steadily flourished, and John even told her he believed they would be married, but Anna kept her own premonitions to herself. One evening before another date, John came in to our place for the first time. He looked around at all of the decor, the furniture, and other belongings in bewilderment, amazed that all of these possessions belonged to one (and a half) person. He asked, "Is all of this stuff yours?" She responded relatively defensively, "Yeah, it is." "Wow, I can fit everything I own into my car." Back then, John was driving a small 280Z sports car. It was then that John got freaked out. Anna was an intelligent woman. She knew exactly what he was trying to say and from then on things weren't the same. John left shortly after for a trip and got cold feet. All he could see now was a bunch of "stuff." He was used to being independent and enjoying his freedom. In college he was in a Christian fraternity, and some of his closest brothers swore by their motto, "Bachelor 'til the Rapture." When he got back, he informed my mother that they should just be friends. They then spent the better part of a year avoiding each other at church.

A year later momma was still on his heart, and he couldn't shake it. He went to his small group leader's home to pray for what he was sure would be a release from his original notions of marriage to her. Instead, what he got when they all prayed individually was a strong urging that Anna was in fact the one that was to be his wife. Around the same period, unannounced to John, Anna had become dismayed by their lack of any communication. She was sure that she'd heard God speak to her about him before. There was a special offering held the previous Sunday, and she emptied essentially everything she had in her bank account, two hundred dollars, as a sacrifice to her obedience to any direction she was supposed to go, so long as she got some sort of confirmation regarding which direction to head.

John was in a near panic trying to figure out what he should do. He begged for advice from his mentors as to where to begin with her again, and was met with the intelligent response, "Start by asking her out, dummy." John was sure that she didn't care about him one way or the other, certain she was more than happy to do whatever she had to do to raise me alone, and that she didn't need someone else's apprehensions. In spite of this, he gathered up the guts to call. It was a Thursday evening. He tried to set up a date that Friday night. She said she already had plans. He said, "Cancel them." She refused, but he wasn't deterred. He understood she had waited patiently, but had gotten tired of the long pause in his pursuit. He called around looking for her, and learning that she was at the home of a mutual friend, he drove directly there to tell her how he felt. Both of them broke down their defenses in recognition of their calling for one another. They held each other in agreement and cried together.

Shortly thereafter, John left for a trip to the Cayman Islands with his family. This time there were no cold feet. He boldly told them he was getting married (which was slightly difficult since he'd hardly even spoken of Anna to any of his relatives). Asking for permission from Papa Al was even better. The two men—of completely different backgrounds—went into a back room where my grandfather asked him two important questions. When Papa Al spoke John's name, he uses a very distinctive tone. It is almost like he is questioning a mischievous child caught in the act of something. Papa Al's voice spikes and holds each letter in sustained raspy suspense.

"Now JOoohhn, do you have a good job?"

"Yes sir, I do."

"Will Anna have to work anymore?"

"No sir."

"Okay. Good enough for me."

When he returned, he proposed on a romantic train ride and asked her how long she would need to plan a wedding. They were married in the church where we had all met on January 6, 1990. I was three and a half. John told me that he never had any fear of the complications our union might present. He was ready to consider me completely as his own, but was terrified about not knowing what to do in marriage or in fatherhood. In the end, he said his fears were alleviated by his obedience to God's word, and the assurance that his diligence would be rewarded with everything he needed to succeed along the way. To pledge his devotion to our new family, he made vows to my mother at the altar as a husband, and separate vows to me as a father. He knew I was never going to leave her side, and we all walked down the aisle together on the way out.

Momma had the last laugh. She said her sacrifice shortly before brought her significant gains, and that she had purchased her husband for only two hundred bucks.

Chapter 3

The Son Who Ran from God

Feeling continuously blessed by the advancement of their lives, my mom and new dad began to feel called to the ministry. The time leading up to their marriage was a tender and formative age for me. There was never any contention that I simply had two dads, but there was a different sort of conflict for me in the way I was raised. Under the headship of a wonderful man and pastor, John was offered a full-time position in the church, allowing him to resign from his post at the bank. My parents were eager to make the right impression on me, but were slightly on the crazy side of a righteous quest. *Ghostbusters* was a huge hit film back then, but I was not allowed to have the coolest new green "slime" juice box from the movie's goofy character, because of the film's affiliation with ghosts and the demonic realm. I was not allowed to watch the children's show *Eureeka's Castle* because of the magic, which was suggestive of sorcery and witchcraft. And after the *Karate Kid* series and subsequent martial arts spin-offs, kicking butt was all the craze among youngsters, but I was not allowed to take lessons because my parents feared that the classes would expose me to alternative religions. I didn't feel as dismayed by not being able to partake in these activities, as I was confused as to why they were forbidden. My parents said later that they didn't understand their own reasoning at the time, except that they were young and trying to raise their first child together. They admitted that they made strange, clueless errors just trying to be good parents, and, felt that they had to go through their own trials in an attempt to get it right, like anybody else.

On the other hand, I got to spend every other weekend with my biological father in a completely different household. My mother was fully aware each exertion they had made to instill wholesome Christian values was subject to instant reversal as I walked out of their door and into his. She said it was heartbreaking to watch me leave every time, but had made a conscious decision to never say a poor word about my father in front of me. She was determined to allow me to love my father for who he was.

At my father's home, it seemed that there was almost always someone else around. Usually at his place, the party consisted of the many "uncle types" I grew up with: Bones, Fish, Cat Daddy, B, Parvis, and Rod. If they weren't all at the house, my father would occasionally take me to meet up with them to listen to some live music. Several times he even made me a part of the legendary night scene of 6th Street—I sat on a tall stool at a round-top table drinking root beer from a bottle to emulate equality with the guys. There was also his long-term crazy girlfriend. She was always caring toward me, but she had the tendency to be eccentric and sporadically emotional, which led to some terrible shouting matches between them. She had a daughter who was about the same age as me. For the sake of companionship, I tolerated her when we were forced to stay in the back room together after a certain point during the parties, but mostly she disgusted and annoyed me to no end.

My favorite memories with him are the few when it was just us; the occasions in the car listening to Eric Clapton and The Eagles, and (our shared favorite) the greatest hits album of Tom Petty and the Heartbreakers. Every so often there was a quiet and calm Friday night; he'd always order a Mr. Ghatti's pizza (the source of my steadfast loyalty to their pies). I also liked the Saturday mornings when he'd wake me up for a joy ride in his white BMW with its sheepskin seat covers. All of the windows and sunroof would be open, and he'd blare the song "Free Fallin'" over and over. We'd wear matching shades, and my little arm hung out in the breeze as we cruised the city streets. I've never felt cooler than I did during those rides alone in the front seat with my dad. We ended up at the same breakfast eatery, The Omelettry, with the same frequency as our pizza choice. There were no filters on his or his friends' demeanor or discourse. I was allowed to watch virtually whatever I wanted, including R-rated movies, and I never had to get dressed up or go to church on Sundays. In a child's eyes, he was the quintessential cool guy. I was living, seeing, and hearing things way beyond my years, and somehow it all seemed normal, like every other kid on the block had the same experiences growing up.

Once he dropped me off though, it was back to rules and regulations, values and structure. These were pounded into me, with the hope that they'd overcome the voice perched on my other shoulder whispering into my ear. What a terrible position it must have been for John having to play the role opposite that of Mr. Fun. But he stood his ground alongside my mother, and I am proud to say that I have never once challenged him in the rebellious context of, "You're not my real dad," because he never treated me as anything less than his real son, and I subsequently never viewed him in any other light.

Meanwhile, back on the home front, my parents' diligence with their church duties was paying off, and they were given more and more responsibilities. A friend and affiliate of the church they were serving was trying to start up his own church in the Cayman Islands, and he needed some sort of "all-purpose" assistant to help. John was capable of handling all of the finances from his days in the bank and leading worship with his voice and piano skills. When he was approached for the position, he asked for some time to go home and pray about it with my mom. He liked the place and comfort they were in and wanted to take the decision seriously. But when he asked her to pray with him, he said she closed her eyes, put her head down, and popped back up just as quickly, saying, "Yep, I prayed about it. That's where we're supposed to go!" Now with a fresh addition to our family, my little sister Hilary, we all uprooted for seven glorious months on the beaches of Grand Cayman Island.

Upon our return to the mainland, we settled back in Austin, but we didn't stay there long either. My parents had been going back and forth between two churches springing up in two small towns, and they were approached again with a position in Waco, Texas. We were part of a neat church (no, nothing to do with the Branch Davidians and David Koresh) that practiced Christianity with a different approach than most; with truly open arms. "Invite them all," we'd say. Bring in the ones nobody else wants. Bring in the drug addicts, those who have never found a welcoming home before, and especially those who believed they were beyond salvation, so we could inform them otherwise.

Those were some of the best times. The pastor's family, some of his longtime friends and fellow staff members, and our family all lived on the same street in a row of duplexes. The first family had six kids, the other four, and we now had three with the addition of my new brother Christian. The doors were always open for people to fill the air on our street and in the church, which was rapidly growing. Dress up or down, it didn't matter there. The only focus was on God, and trying to spread His message however it could best be applied. We had a free carnival encouraging each member to bring at least one friend who didn't attend church, our own scary house on Halloween (that was good enough to put the fear of God back into people while trying to save them from hell), and a "Cycle Sunday" with several real motorcycles riding down the aisles for the faithfully attending leather-clad bikers who wanted their friends to come as well.

Two years after Christian, we welcomed the final addition to our loving family, sweet little Rachel. It was as if each new child was a sign of the growth taking place in my parents' lives, their dedication to their faith, and the increasing prosperity they were passing down to us both physically and spiritually. I say this because while our own family was growing, so were the number of young people involved with the church. Despite what people might have said about the parenting of my biological father, and some of the unsettling circumstances I had experienced with him at a young age by fundamentalists standards, good nonetheless prevailed. All of my parents truly wanted the best for me. A youth group was being organized, its core was being established by a great group of kids, and I was happy to be a part of it.

To my parents' joy, I had taken a very strong role in the youth group's development. Under the direction of Anthony, an awesome youth leader, and following the same platform as "big church," we came up with our own unique ways to bring young students in. I'm not very fond of the sayings, "it's fate," or "everything happens for a reason," but I do believe that everything does have its place and purpose in the universe void of chance. Anthony and I were connected before we ever knew it. Our fathers knew one another through another form of connection, and had partied together a lot in the past. Their two sons were now choosing a very different path. Anthony was one of my best friends and greatest mentors through pivotal times for me. He was there for everything, even to bust me under the stairs by the sanctuary with the first girl I kissed, who was older, in the middle of seventh grade. I had never done anything to get into any real trouble before and was a mess when he forced me to man up and tell my parents what I had done before he did. It was right before my little brother Christian's birthday, and I was looking for any excuse to postpone what I thought would be a severe punishment.

Standing in front of my mom and dad sitting calmly in bed behind closed doors, they said, "Well go on with it. What do you have to tell us?" I finally let it out, "Alright, I kissed Jamie Sullivan under the stairs at church. I'm so sorry." They looked at one another with a straight face, looked back at me, and prolonged the suspense until I could hardly take it. "Just yell at me already, ground me, whatever, but say something!!!" I screamed to myself inside. Then my mom spoke, and I realized the silence was much better. Without breaking character she said in the most tranquil voice, "You know why guys name their penises, right?" I was *completely* thrown off guard. The room was spinning. "Where did this come from? What is happening to me?" "No mom. Why?" "Because they don't like taking orders from strangers." Before I even had a chance to comprehend what she had said, my dad, John (usually mild-mannered and well-spoken), proved even he had his own humorous flare for shock value. With the same placid look, he asked, "Did you get a boner?" I was mortified.

Inside, they must have been rejoicing over their excellent tag-teaming of my mind (while keeping a straight face), but I was ready for it to be over and to get on with my anticipated punishment. What they said next never fully registered, but I never fully forgot it either. I just wanted them to yell, tell me I messed up, or that they were disappointed, but instead they showed me gentle grace and explained the concept of "soul ties" for the first time. I had no idea what "soul ties" were. They said the physical act of intimacy binds your heart and soul to the person you are sharing it with, thus emotionally tying you to them, and giving that portion of your heart away which can't be returned. They were tying this all into a "no sex before marriage" speech, but I had gotten defensive in my argument that it was just a kiss and that I was only thirteen with no thoughts or intentions of having sex. Their concern was I was already oblivious to the path I was now on, and worried that pieces of my heart would be given away to too many people with too little left for the one it all should be saved for. I shrugged it all off.

During the two years after that little chitchat my faith grew, and the goal of the youth group was to prepare us for the hardships of all of the many temptations we would soon be flooded with. Having started high school, we were in a new phase at the church, and I was asked to be a part of a new leadership team. Members would have to successfully graduate from a training course, as well as take an oath for a life of purity to set a guiding example for the rest of our peers. In the beginning, I was fully on board. However, the guiltlessness I felt for seemingly small acts, such as the kiss, soon gave way to a swinging door I was now willing to sway situationally with. I was unable to see, as my parents could, what my behavior might mean further down the road.

The closeness of that road was as figurative as it was literal. Just down the street, my friends and I were forming a group of our own. Things were pretty great. I had a really pretty girlfriend I enjoyed spending time with and an assortment of vagabonds, about eight of us altogether, with whom I spent the rest. It was the summer, and the guys and I were enjoying playing football, getting into casual trouble here and there, and throwing our first party when one of the member's fathers went out of town on business. We passed a plastic bottle of cheap liquor around the room, listened to loud music, and laughed the night away. We didn't get hangovers, didn't attract any attention from our parents, and the feeling was that there was nothing wrong with what we were doing once in a blue moon. At the turn of our sophomore year though, the business trips became more frequent, and so did our parties.

I believe all decisions coincide with others. Along with the increasing frequency of our drinking, my relationship with my girlfriend had turned into an all-out physical exploration. I had come to a constrained moment of consummation; a point that could no longer justify the convictions needed to avoid flexing morally. My priorities were shifting, and my attention had been re-directed. In the middle of a Wednesday night service, I was asked to pray for someone else's vices, and I cringed at the thought of positioning myself between the hypocrisies of Christianity. I had once heard a verse to the effect that God spews the lukewarm from his mouth. I hated the idea of a double life, and I hated the idea of playing holy. I couldn't excuse pretenses now that my choices were clear. The parties were taking place every weekend. To the PTA moms who were catching wind of our stories, we were known as "the booze crew" and a menace. To everyone else in school we were simply known as "the group". Among the youth group, I began to sit in the back. I began to fall off the map. I had effectively left one group for another.

Chapter 4

Hurting for Mommy

Two days before Valentine's Day during my freshman year of college, my life seemingly began to fall apart. By the end of high school, all of the partying was spiraling out of control. I knew if I stuck with my friends once we left home I wouldn't make it through the first year in a major university. Instead, I focused more attention on my longtime on-again off-again girlfriend to stay out of trouble. Our relationship was ultimately terrible. We fought. We brought out the worst in each other. We were passionate when things were good and even more passionate when they weren't (which seemed to become a greater amount of the time). No matter what happened though, we always returned to start the cycle over again. We were trapped. It was the kind of trap everyone could see except for the people in it, because the participants have their blinders on at all times. It was the kind of trap that is all too common and inescapable by those who fall into them. It finally ended in lies. It ended in deceit. It ended in complete brokenness for both parties after I walked in on her and a third party. It ended in anger, bitterness, harsh words, and tears. She was my first love.

I told myself I would never speak to her again. I told myself I would never allow her into my life again. I told myself I would not get caught in that trap again. I had stumbled across an alternative way of making money that was conducive to my school schedule. I was doing clinical research studies; yes, guinea-pig stuff. The studies paid really well, but while I participated, I had to stay in the research facility for the entire duration, usually going through the weekend, or several days. One study took place for around five days during my spring break, and while there were two movie rooms, a pool table and an internet room, this type of life can quickly get claustrophobic. I had too much free time, and my mind was wandering to awful places. It had only been a few weeks since I had sworn her off after the great betrayal, and I missed her. I sat in the most private place I could find and asked myself a sincere and honest question, "Why?" I knew the truth. I knew she was not someone I wanted to be with for the rest of my life, so why was I longing for her again and prepared to overlook anything to work it all out? The answer was simple. It had been hidden for years, waiting to emerge and say, "I told you so." It was the soul ties my parents had warned me about years before. We had given too much of our hearts to the wrong person, and now they were wrapped in a stranglehold. Our alleged need for one another had nothing to do with love, but everything to do with premature intimacy, jealousy, and imaginary authenticity. I was wrecked; not by pain anymore, but by guilt. I had spent the last four years running from my parent's teachings, and this is where it had gotten me.

When I checked out of the study I stayed with my best friend, and one of the members of "the group." We enjoyed hanging out as guys, but I had a phone call to make. I was hurting for my mommy. It was late, and I was sitting outside in the dark on a third-floor balcony overlooking the city. Besides being my mother, Anna was a wonderful listener and amazingly insightful. She was the only person I would go to for matters of the heart. Her voice alone spread a warm presence around you, it was the comforting cradle only a mother is capable of. From one hundred miles away I broke in her arms. For years I had acted in unrestricted rebellion toward my parents. I was on my own agenda. I had done what I wanted when I wanted, yelled back at their opposition, disrespected their home, and jeopardized their reputation. I left them in an impossible situation as to what to do with me. I was one of the kids who leaves his parents feeling hopeless and wondering where they went wrong. Something finally clicked. The selfishness dissipated, and I poured out the depths of my soul to her with the most forthright conversation we had ever shared. I told her about all of the drinking, the wrong turns, and the misery it had brought upon me. I told her I was ashamed of the way I had treated them, and how appreciative I was that they had stood by me. I told her I was sorry. I even told her about the pregnancy scare I had, and how my girlfriend and I were faced with the worst feeling in the wake of the decision we might have had to make. It turned out to be nothing more than a scare, but also nothing short of an awakening. I asked her how she ever managed to have and raise me, essentially by herself. I told her that I felt terrible for ever making that seem like a poor choice on her end and for her willingness to sacrifice her life for a son who wasn't willing to repay her for what she'd given up.

I deserved crossed arms and a furiously tapping foot. I deserved to be yelled at and slapped. I did not, however, deserve the unbelievable grace she showed me once again, and the words that comprise the most cherished conversation I ever had with her. She told me she revealed her pregnancy with me to her family just before Christmas, and that they were livid. They locked her in her room and gave her a dictionary as a present—the book was to reinforce their wish for her to stay in school and avoid ruining her life. She was barely twenty-one years old. She was told she would be disowned if she went against them and had me. She was alone, scared, and crying her eyes out in bed when she said she heard God's voice for the first time in her life. He calmly said to her with an assuring authority, "Anna, you don't have a choice. You don't have a choice." I heard all of this for the first time in complete amazement. She went on to explain that immediately after, she dried her eyes and knew she had no choice but to be obedient. She was relieved of her worries and walked with the sense that any of our needs would be met, and any obstacles would somehow be overcome.

I was in awe of her strength and in disbelief that the texture of her being was so smooth; void of any scars or chips on her shoulders. I was not upset in the least that my potential existence was once disputed. I was overcome with an overwhelming obligation to do something important with my life so as to repay the debts of her diligence to me and to God. After listening to this story, our relationship reached a completely new level of closeness and unabashed openness. It was clear to me that I was allowed into this world with an intention for a very specific purpose. It wasn't until my last semester of college, three years later, that I was sure I had discovered my purpose. The usual questions were swirling around my graduation as to what I would do with the degree we had spent so much money to attain. I was in Hawaii at the time, and as we spoke over a distance of four thousand miles, the subject of my future plans was lightly brought up. The day before she had told me my younger brother, Christian, had spoken some very kind words about something I had written and posted online. She was not exactly a technology guru, so she asked me to e-mail some of my writings directly. Coming back to the question she had posed before, I asked if she had read the creative pieces I had sent. "Yes I did. They were beautiful." "Thank you, Mother. That is my answer. I am going to be a writer." "I know son, I read your work. It is definitely what you have been called to do.

I believe in you, and hope God uses you to change the world. Now go do it."

If in the very least we are reduced to words, what a blessing it is to be able to use them to glorify her life now, and her one decision to obey the word of God. I can't say enough about how much I respect and love her.

Chapter 5

Specifically for the Non-Believers

I have to change course for just a moment to ensure I don't lose certain audiences with all of the Jesus talk. To maintain the accuracy of my mother's message, and the way she would want her heart to be portrayed, I will not withhold her firm devotion to Christianity. I will be speaking of some all-encompassing principles she embodied that one might be in agreement with. I acknowledge and respect that there are many people who do not believe in theories of creationism. I'm also aware that many people are severely struggling with their faith, especially those who've suffered a tragedy. I do not wish to appear self-righteous, claim to have consistently shown as a beacon of holiness, nor do I intend to speak any judgment, but I do wish to offer some alternative views to establish a middle ground before you put this book down.

Despite growing up in the church, like anybody, I too have struggled with these immense concepts. I remember taking a philosophy course one summer.

The professor asked the entire class of about thirty students to raise their hands if they believed in God. Only two people did so; myself and one other girl. I felt horrible for her. She had a thick southern accent that was innocent, and quickly gave away the fact that she had never even been in a situation in which the existence in heaven was questioned. With her dropped jaw, she was an easy target, immediately exploited by the man at the head of the class. I was hung over, and probably appeared less inviting for a fight. He singled her out and told her to give her best argument in favor of her beliefs. She was quivering and unprepared, playing right into his bullying tactics. The professor then began to rip the Bible apart starting with the story of Noah's Ark. "C'mon guys," he said, "How stupid is it to believe that a one hundred-year-old man could build a ship big enough to house two of every animal on earth for forty days and nights and provide all that they would need to eat. Not to mention cleaning up the amount of feces, which would have rapidly spread diseases killing them all!" People were laughing at his rehearsed punch lines and condescending style. She was shrinking in her seat. I was angry at his unprofessionalism and the way he made me so critically question this concept, though the last laugh was on him. His life was clearly not all that he would have wished. He was balding, told us about his failed marriage and was blatantly bitter that the University of Texas had refused to renew his contract to teach there; obviously unable to cope with being reduced to summer courses at a community college.

Dissenters like him, which take every opportunity to make people feel belittled for their beliefs, are not the only people I am upset with. I am equally upset with the church itself for painting the wrong picture of Christ's image. I like to paraphrase two concepts: one from a brilliant pastor, and the other from a youth minister and accredited author whom I am proud to call a friend. To preface in my own terms: I hate when people say to me, "Oh, you're religious?" to confirm that I believe in a higher being. This terminology reflects a problem in our society's viewpoints that too often go unchecked. To be clear, yes, I do believe in God, but I do not necessarily believe in religion. And, no, they are *not* one and the samc. In John 14:6, Jesus says, "*I* am the way, the truth, and the life. No one comes to the Father except through *me*." In its many varieties, religion instigates customs and personal interpretations that have arguably led to many losing focus on the core foundation of Jesus's teachings. They also fail to heed His warning in Matthew 5:20, "But I warn you, unless you obey God better than the teachers of religious law and the Pharisees, you can't enter the Kingdom of Heaven at all!"

The Pharisees were the ultimate "religious" people of the biblical day. They projected themselves as the final voice and determining standard of divinity. They were also some of the first to cast judgment, a right reserved for only one deity. Over hundreds of years, the Pharisees tried to attain the highest level of religiosity in preparation for the coming of Christ. They longed to be worthy in His presence upon His arrival, but lost focus of their motives somewhere along the way. They held a steadfast view of what they thought Jesus was going to be like, and when he finally came though, he was nothing close to what they had imagined. While the Pharisees had taken every effort to ostracize to damnation the beggars, the diseased, the prostitutes, and every other sinner, Jesus showed them mercy, grace, and forgiveness. It was in His humility and love for the most downtrodden members of society that Jesus was able to connect with everyone (except for the judgmental), and the Pharisees hated him for it. They hated him so much, that they were the ones responsible for his death.

It baffles me how often the church forgets the essence of Jesus and His ability to connect, all while claiming to teach His lessons. It saddens me to no end to see those trying to do his work miss the point so badly. I've come out of bars, concerts, and college campuses only to hear some radical nut screaming into a megaphone with a correlating message on a sign saying everyone is a sinner and going to burn in hell for eternity. I can't help but wonder whether he took the opportunity to connect and show mercy before starting on his rant. I see the alienation of young people who are attacked by those attempting to represent Jesus this way. I see the false views that are forever burned into souls that could have been saved had they not been made to feel they had to fit into a specific category of dress, ideology, and character to enter the walls of the Lord. What happened to come one and come all? I believe religion has become critically disconnected from those it purports to serve. It is no wonder that the highest officials in our religious institutions are falling to charges of horrendous accusations, and people don't want to be associated in any way with the modern day Pharisees of Christianity.

I say, whatever your religious affiliation, let us get back to a place of connection and inclusion, and put a stop to all of these religious wars. I also realize some people like structure, while others need something a bit more unorthodox. Whatever your needs may be, I encourage you to find a church that is right for you. And to my mind, the church that is right for anyone must accept your imperfections while pushing you to have a personal relationship with the Lord that has room to grow and flourish.

I would urge you to not fall to tradition. While we often regard tradition fondly during fun events and holidays, we often just go through repetitive practices without questioning the origins of our actions. Tied to tradition, we stay within the comfortable confines of parameters set in eras that likely do not relate to current times, and have not been allowed to progress into practices that can sustain us today. Our lives are constantly changing, and we experience more than physical and mental growth. Spiritual maturity must also take place and not be stagnated by tradition and strict religious restrictions. How are we ever supposed to continue sculpting ourselves into chiseled warriors defending God's kingdom if we haven't taken the necessary steps to equip ourselves against seasoned attacks?

I say, find the formula that works for you. If your relationships on earth don't grow, they fall apart. Why wouldn't that be any different with God? Love Him well, strive for more, defy the boundaries of spiritual minimalism, and be bold in your daily walk. Tread lightly in your assumptions about others so you do not fall to extreme misunderstandings. Much like there is an intended separation of church and state, there must be a separation of what the Lord says to you and what you want His words to mean. Stay connected to your calling and to your neighbor, be accepting of everyone's views, and live life diligently in an effort to better humanity. Read what Jesus had to say at the end of the book of Matthew and determine for yourself what He was clearly asking of us:

> Some Pharisees and teachers of religious law arrived from Jerusalem to interview Jesus. "Why do your disciples disobey our age-old traditions?" they demanded. "They ignore our tradition of ceremonial hand washing before they eat."
>
> Jesus replied, "And why do you, by your traditions, violate the direct commandments of God? For instance, God says, 'Honor your

father and mother,' and 'Anyone who speaks evil of father or mother must be put to death [according to the Old Testament].' But you say, 'You don't need to honor your parents by caring for their needs if you give the money to God instead.' And so, by your own tradition, you nullify the direct commandment of God. You hypocrites! Isaiah was prophesying about you when he said, 'These people honor me with their lips, but their hearts are far away.'

Their worship is a farce, for they replace God's commandments with their own man-made teachings" (Matthew 15:1–11).

Chapter 6

The Life of Forgiveness

Two of Jesus's greatest qualities were grace and forgiveness, and my mother emulated them well. She definitely showed me an abundance of both, but it took a tough life lesson to see these attributes in her. She showed me how much life there is in forgiveness, and that although it is much easier for our pride to hold a grudge, doing so is very difficult on our spirits.

When I was in the eighth grade I went into my parents' office to grab a peppermint I had seen before heading out the door on the way to a concert. On the desk was a typed speech my mom had been preparing for a women's conference in Peru. I had walked in while she was writing it the night before to ask her a question, but was quickly shooed away when she noticed my curiosity about her project. She told me I was not allowed to read her speech and once again told me to scram.

As no one was home, I tried to quickly skim over the document as my friends were outside honking the horn. I only saw one word, "adultery." Without being able to see the context surrounding that single term I was overcome with fear, doubt, confusion, and a crazed concern as to what she was alluding to. Infidelity had always seemed impossible between my parents, and now I was flooded with terrible thoughts that needed to be resolved immediately.

The next opportunity that arose, I was scouring the office in search of answers. She had removed the physical copy, but the saved document took almost no time to find. It turned out to be a brilliant and self-exposing message addressing the needs of every woman who had been hurt and abused. Unfortunately, her tale was told out of experience, and those unwelcomed experiences came from my biological father; the fun guy who I had always glorified. The point was to shed light on the pitfalls of poor relationships, along with the hope of redemption and salvation after breaking free of the devastation. To establish her legitimacy, she wrote candid accounts of the emotional voids in her heart after losing her mother at such a young age, and the resulting blind desire for love to try to fill those gaps when it seemed no one else was there for her. The "adultery" she spoke of came from her strong conviction to give herself to only one man. No matter what he put her through, leaving him was not an option for her. Loyalty was one of her strongest attributes. She was committed to him. Anything else, in her mind, made her unredeemable, tainted, and an adulterer. She endured all of these wounds despite her knowledge of my father's habitual drug use and dealing, frequent verbal torments, and his affairs with other women.

Her conclusion was that they were not right for each other, and that she was still worthy of happiness and love in God's eyes. She had achieved this on her own. First, she was virtuously cleansed by God's grace after finding the ability to escape from the strong holds of her own soul ties. Later, she found everything she deserved in John. My mother had tried to protect me from this information out of her respect for and forgiveness of my biological father, knowing full well he was still my dad, and that I loved him. But I had sought this info out on my own, and was then confused and hurt.

I was in junior high, which are awkward times for everyone. These years present all of us with our first life crisis, searching for who we are while juggling the many pressures that seem to come from all angles. For me, nothing made any sense. I was in the school band and on the football team. I was trying to be attractive amidst the first battles with acne, and like everyone else, I was struggling to find acceptance while avoiding the rejection that seemed to lurk around every corner. The last thing I needed was to begin questioning my dad's love for me. I never told my mom what I had done, never discussed anything with my dad, and proceeded to let it all tear me to shreds inside for the better part of a year.

Around that time, my mother's sister, Aunt Junie, became ill. Before long, her sickness had turned into pneumonia, and the situation quickly grew dim. Having checked into the hospital, the status of her condition was downgraded to "grave." Junie was in a coma and silently fighting for her life. However, my mom was there with her to refuse anything except her survival. She immediately packed a bag and made the short trek south to Austin to be by her side, leaving my three siblings and I in the sole care of our father, John, for over a week.

During this period, Momma stayed by the bed in the ICU after visiting hours, beyond personal comfort, beyond the clutches of doubt, and beyond the bounds of love for another. She was well equipped and ready. She had Post-it notes with specific scriptures all over the wall. She repeatedly read aloud a narrative on healing like a proud child reading his first book. When her voice finally tired, she popped in a tape with an encouraging voice preaching the same healing sermon. At times, when others came to visit, she would preface their presence with a stern demand for positivity before they were permitted. She absolutely refused to allow anything negative to enter the life of the restorative force field she had built.

The mind usually only acts upon what it can visibly see. The prognosis was simple, "She's not going to make it." For those who had come to visit Junie, that message was what they saw. I think the logical thing for everyone to do was to start preparing an emotional support for Anna for when the monitors inevitably flatlined. Someone should have prepared them for her tenacity though. When friends and family called just to ask how Junie was doing, they were baffled when she happily said, "Oh she's great! She's getting better every day."

Factually, she was still in a coma and had made no visible progress. The contradicting voices left many visitors confused and slightly worried that my mother was delusional and unable to handle the reality of the medical severity. Momma Rambeau, however, was working on faith that far exceeded worldly interpretations. Junie's doctor later had to retract his prediction. He said there was no reasonable explanation for Aunt Junie's survival. He said, in essence, "Call it luck, random chance, or call it a miracle, but she should not be alive today, and she is. It had little, if anything, to do with medicine."

My Uncle Bill was the only brother surrounded by three sisters. When he was around, he was an absolute riot; he always had a beer in hand and a raunchy laugh to match his jokes. For the majority of holidays and family gatherings though, he was nonexistent and bitter. In spite of his conspiracy theories about not being invited, he had created the disconnection himself. It is unclear as to when his miscalculations began. His feelings of inadequacy obviously set in at an early age, causing him to lash out in a behavioral pattern resembling a family's typical black sheep. Along the way he became irretrievably adrift.

When Bill was particularly screwed up on hard drugs, he would call to curse my mother. These were foul rants completely disengaged from reality;

he spoke in a low, grumbling tenor, mixing threats with accusations that she hated him. They were the kind of belittling berates that were directly meant to inflict unforgivable pain.

One day I received a phone call from my mom explaining that Uncle Bill was in the hospital and asking me to go visit him immediately. He had been there for two weeks without telling anyone. He had adamantly told the nurses that he had no family, and his siblings only found out because he had no health insurance. This caused the hospital staff to do some digging, and they uncovered his false claims of abandonment.

I don't understand people who reject others in an attempt to further their own rejection, but Uncle Bill's eyes lit up the second I walked into his room. True to form, he was in the middle of telling his nurse a dirty joke, but he was quick to give me a welcoming introduction as one of his beloved own. It was clear he loved the familiar company, despite his efforts to keep us out.

I said, "Hey, Uncle Bill, what's wrong with you?" The only information my mom had been given was that he had slipped in the shower and was having complications from diabetes—his leg had swollen to twice its normal size and wouldn't return to normal. I was caught off guard to hear him casually reply, "Oh, I'm just dying." He just had a busted up leg. How in the world could he think he was dying? It was the end of October, and by early January he was gone.

In a matter of months he wilted, deflated, and transformed from a vibrant middle-aged man to the embodiment of an elderly expired frame. He lost his teeth and the color in his hair. He lost his strength and the ability to walk on his own power. He could no longer take care of himself, and the people who stepped up were those he'd believed to have walked out on him years before. He was put in a nursing home in Waco, enabling my mom to attend to him personally every day. He even made it to church with her on multiple occasions, where mom proudly introduced him as her brother (rather than hiding him in the back with the other embarrassing black-sheep types).

On his deathbed, my mother gave him life. He was finally willing to accept Jesus into his heart at her behest. Holding on to each deep breath, he looked up at her, and said, "Anna, I *am* holy." The way he said it, as though he expected her to denounce him as being a righteous acceptable man like everyone else in his life, hurt her heart. He had set himself up for rejection and in each encounter with others he'd been an outcast in his mind. He had lived a life plagued by mistakes. Although he accepted personal redemption in his final moments, he expected this too to be viewed as another of his abundant failures. Instead, my mother validated his experience. She told him, "Yes, you *are* holy." She saw peace come over his eyes as he slipped back into a comatose state for a few more hours and that is how he left.

He was surrounded by his beginnings, and it was a painful loss. When we left to go home, there were many cars to choose from belonging to all those who had driven into town in time to be with him. Momma decided to ride alone with me. I felt an obligation to say something to her, but the initial "Sorry" clichés seemed unsatisfactory. We sat in silence until the right words suddenly came over me in the middle of a softly playing song.

I explained my notion that Uncle Bill had been under the gripping influence of devastating drugs, and he'd had a hallucinogenic mind-set for decades. His barriers had been impenetrable for the duration of that era, but without access to those drugs, he found the truth. He accepted his family's care and attention, which was only there because they had forgiven him. Despite his death, they had been able to connect with him more intimately over the course of mere months than they had throughout the rest of his life, and Uncle Bill acknowledged and finally appreciated their love.

Already I had learned so much through our family. For years I had grappled with the pains of reading that my mother had caught my dad with another woman when I was only eight months old. Young and emotionally vulnerable, I could not understand why he would forsake our trust at such a tender age. I would wonder why he didn't love me completely, and why my existence wasn't enough to satisfy his desires to stay loyal to my mother and I. It was a lot to take in. I silently forgave him on the basis of nothing more than passing time, but now my uncle's death had brought new clarity.

I looked at how my family had encased my uncle with love. I saw peace in their pain. I thought about how humble they had to be to pardon his former injustices. I also thought about the slab that used to support the frame of the home where my father grew up. He had shown it to me while visiting relatives in that small town once, and shared the story about how his own father was an alcoholic who walked out on his family when my father was only five. He was the youngest of three. His mom worked multiple jobs to keep warm walls around them that were probably no bigger than the single bedroom I enjoyed to myself now. Once his mother was gone, there was no one else to guide him. Naturally, he got into trouble and began to form the habits that would direct a slew of poor decisions later.

We went to visit the estranged man who contributed to my father's birth. I saw the hurt in my father's eyes when he called out the wrong son's name. Finally, I realized he never had a proper image of a real father. I thought about all of the years he had driven every other weekend—three hours each way—to see me. I thought about how he had never missed a home or away game during the ten years I played football (they were all away games for him), and the new jersey he had to buy with my number each time it changed. I thought about how we hold our parents in the light of superheroes, when they are really mere mortal humans; completely capable of making mistakes. For the first time, I knew that

I was forgiving him for the right reason; because I was loved. I realized that his unfortunate upbringing had no bearing on the choices I would have to make in my own life for my future family and myself.

At the root of all of these sentiments, I see the image of my mother. She was created in God's image, and God conceived in her the grace and forgiveness that I take comfort in now.

Texas 4000

Chapter 7

Getting Sick

In the fall of 2006 I heard about an organization called The Texas 4000 for Cancer. With only two days to decide to make a yearlong commitment, fill out the extensive application, and turn in my signed devotion to the cause, I never thought twice about it. Everyone around me said the group was simply too crazy to participate in. As part of the team, the members would be required to attend multiple weekly meetings and raise at least four thousand dollars to be donated collectively at the end of the year to cancer research. We would also need to meet a minimal training regimen, because the next summer we would be riding bicycles from Austin, Texas, to Anchorage, Alaska. You can imagine which part of the commitment most intimidated my peers and questioning family members. Out of hundreds of applicants, fewer than fifty would be selected for the team, and we were told that only around forty people would complete the entire process at the finish line more than four thousand miles away in Alaska.

First hearing about this group only two days prior to the deadline, my paperwork was turned in just before it was all too late. I was fortunate to be interviewed by two former members fresh off the ride. They grilled me on every aspect of my mental toughness, but there wasn't much discussion about any physical requirements. They explained what it would take to ride between eighty and one hundred miles each day, more often than not sleeping on the ground, only to wake up before the sun to do it all again. They explained the aspects that they hadn't foreseen, such as limited cell phone coverage, limited access to showers, and the need to get along well with twenty different people each day, because the ride was split into two different routes. The extended amount of time spent in close contact with other weary souls can easily make way for frustrations that would not normally surface. Apparently, a fight had broken out between two teammates over some Oreo cookies. I assured them that I was a Chips Ahoy fan. Most notably, they explained how necessary it was to connect with the cause on a personal level.

Each morning before leaving they dedicated that day to a different friend, family member, or someone they had met along the way who was battling cancer or had already lost the fight. Yes, there was a certain amount of physical strength required, and that was important, but it did not come close to what it would take to keep your mind pedaling. The idea, they said, was to encase yourself in someone else's shoes. Riding that far seems almost as daunting as surviving cancer at times, but the road to recovery can never be achieved by quitting. If one stops "riding," the repercussion is an actual loss of life. The best way to keep fighting through the hard days on the road was to know someone tenderly. Unfortunately, I never got the chance to meet my grandmother Olivia, but my other grandmother had beaten breast cancer twice. When I received the wonderful news that I had been selected for the team, my grandmothers' courage was what led me to follow through.

I thought my parents would be overjoyed. I was wrong. To my surprise, my mother was an adamant opponent. They wanted me to focus on my studies and graduate on time. "Do it later," they said. They were floored by the idea of taking off an entire summer, along with taking on this huge extracurricular time commitment during the academic year when I was going to school full time and working a part-time job. I heard, in addition, the first hint of cynicism in my mother's voice. She had gone to the hospital too many times to pray for families. She saw people get dropped by their insurance companies with no way to take on the financial burden (easily one hundred fifty thousand to two hundred thousand dollars) of being treated for cancer. She said that she had seen minimal progress in treatment in the nearly thirty years since her mom had died; only fancier machines and higher costs. I had never heard her say anything with such political overtones before, but she actually got pretty worked up. My mind was made up though. There was no such thing as waiting until later for me. I was going to Alaska.

Everyone in my family came around later, when they saw the amount of community involvement the project offered, the sense of passion we had toward life, and a 3.75 GPA for the semester. As with any of my pursuits, my mother became my biggest fan. She was so funny when I was growing up. She always wanted to be involved with what I was doing. She wanted to have my friends over filling the house with our stories and boyish shenanigans, she wanted to be the loudest person in the stadium at my games, and she just wanted to be included in all of my siblings' lives. That summer the route I chose took us straight west to San Francisco, then Highway 1 all the way up the coast, and it wasn't enough for her to hear how pretty my surroundings were or how skinny I had become on the ride. She wanted to be there. As a girl, she remembered a book about the Redwoods, and always wanted to see for herself how immense God's creation could really be. When we made it to Northern California, she and my sister Hilary flew out to see me. After some careful planning, she managed to fly into the closest airport, rented a car, and waited on the side of the road for hours just to see us ride by. We had a day off from riding, and we spent the day driving through that majestic forest.

On the way to dinner that night, my mother got distracted. She stumbled on a rescued seal preserve. In addition to her family and decorating, animals had always been one of her greatest loves. She had worked in a veterinary clinic early on just to be near them. She always knew where the birds' nests were in our yard and helped to shield them from harm. And to my father's dismay, she never turned away a stray dog or cat. She cried and laughed at the same time when she saw this injured seal preserve right on the water. Despite the fact that I was starving, I didn't have a chance of pulling her away from those barking, clapping oceanic teddy bears. She'd never seen seals in person before, and every single time we went somewhere we had to make a *quick* stop by that preserve. If you had seen her face those couple of days, you would have gone hungry too.

We were heading into Oregon the next day. Momma said, "Oh, I want to go to Oregon too! It's not that far. I can make it to the border with you in time to get back for my flight!" The money we had raised also funded the trip's operating costs. In order to keep them to a minimum, and maximize our contribution in the end, we would seek out food donations in each town. We needed a massive amount of sustenance to replenish the energy we were constantly burning. Without it, we would quickly pass out from exhaustion. Once again, Momma wanted to be included in our affairs, and she arranged a rest stop for us like we had explained from food she was able to get donated by a local grocery store. For that day, she was part of the team. At the Oregon border we parted ways, but not without her letting us know how thrilled she was for following through in the present, and not waiting for an opportunity in the future at a "more appropriate time" (that would undoubtedly never come.) We exchanged much joy, and then she left.

In the morning, we woke to our typical routine when one of the girls on our team received a special e-mail. The message contained a video honoring a woman that the girl had befriended through another service organization. The video's subject had recently passed away from cancer. There was some live footage, but the rest was mostly a compilation of photos of her last few days in the hospital. The woman was surrounded by an abundance of family, and she was all smiles. One of the last images was the most compelling as it quickly passed. It was a poster board covered with get-well cards. In the very center was a hand-drawn card from her young daughter, who could not have been more than five years old. The image has haunted me ever since. In a squiggly, unsteady, innocent child's penmanship it read, "Don't Die Mommy." Mere hours removed from my mother, I quietly excused myself from the group, still huddled over the computer screen and sat sobbing uncontrollably in a restroom stall. At some point all of our team was unforgettably touched by one moment or another during the trip. Many had already had their moment. This was mine. I shattered into pieces for the little girl in those pictures made forever motherless by a senseless disease. I shattered for the same little girl that was my mother years before. And I cried tears of joy that I still had mine. I felt so ashamed for ever taking her for granted, and I felt more blessed than ever that she did not have to endure the struggle with the disease that I was riding for. At that time, I had no idea of what was to come.

When we returned home from the incredible journey to Alaska I was unable to stay at the community college in Austin, and unwilling to return to the university thirty miles south where I had spent my freshman year. Therefore, I did what any sensible person would do in a similar situation. I transferred to the University of Hawaii. Despite being a week removed from the bike, a week late for classes, having no friends in a place I'd never before been, or even a place to live; going to Hawaii was easy. The only hard part, like with the Texas 4000 for Cancer, was convincing my parents that it was the right decision in the beginning. Of course, they were not very pleased with my choice or distance from them. They tried to keep me from going, but too often arguments of this magnitude turn to bitter sentiments of a child conceptualizing their parents conspiring to ruin their lives by not letting them do something. I on the other hand, now see a parent's instinct to protect their child above all else. To a parent, acceptable choices are often those decisions with the least possible risk; mine were anything but. I did prevail, however, and within a week I managed to find my own place (escaping the hostel and random person's couch, where I'd slept each night). I made priceless friends and quickly flourished, eagerly getting involved with more service organizations. For me, it was truly the best place I could have ever gone.

Shortly after moving to Hawaii, a good friend of mine offered to take me anywhere in the world that I wanted to go. She had a travel scholarship that had to be used up by Christmas, and also had connections in the airlines. I chose Thailand. She said she didn't want to go to Thailand. I said, "Okay, you pick then." She settled on Budapest, Hungary. I'd moved to Hawaii with no more than I could comfortably carry on my own to easily navigate those unknown streets (two small bags and a guitar I didn't know how to play at the time). Wearing board shorts and flip-flops every day, I wasn't exactly prepared for Eastern Europe in the dead of winter. This required a phone call home to explain my Christmas plans halfway across the world (and to ask my parents to send some heavy coats). There was no rush on the care package though, and life resumed as normal for a while.

The same friend and I took a small, preliminary excursion to the island of Maui, but on the plane ride home something came over my spirit that I could not shake. It lasted for days, and I could not interpret the feeling any further than an indescribably overwhelming need to return home once classes were finished. Since this notion had nothing to do with being homesick, it seemed best to be obedient to the feeling. The only hitch was that it was November, my family was already set on me leaving the country for the holidays, and I didn't want to deviate from that plan so late in the game only to have to ask for money for a plane ticket with the sky rocketing prices for flights. There was a special one-way fare going to San Francisco, and it was the only affordable option back to the mainland. The other half of the trip remained unplanned, but I figured I'd have a jacket and, if need be, a few days to hitchhike to Texas, before Christmas Day arrived. That was the informal plan, and I was the only one who knew of its existence.

The week of finals, Momma called me as I was walking back home from campus. There was nothing unusual about her tone when she asked about my day and how my exams were going. She then continued, "Hey, I sent you that box with warmer clothes. Oh, and we got a call from the doctor's office today. I know you're leaving soon, and don't want you to worry on your trip, but I found out I have breast cancer." She said they had caught it early, and that she was having a mastectomy in less than two weeks. She said, "We're going to take this thing head-on, and I'm going to beat it. Everything's going to be fine. God is on my side, and I will come out victorious!" In spite of my mother's positive outlook, it took everything inside of me to keep from collapsing in that courtyard. Surrounded by sprawling palm trees and warm sea breezes, I stood frozen by the news. Back in my room, the tears flowed. Initially, there were only two people I could confide in: one was Katherine. I had been patiently pursuing her for a year and a half trying to balance friendship with underlying emotions that had gone unsaid due to the instabilities of a vagabond; the other was Ty. Ty was my best friend since childhood, when we lived across the street from each other.

The summer after graduating high school, years before, Ty called me one day and said, "Dude I need to ask you something crazy." I stopped him before he could finish responding, "Whatever it is, I want you to know, I'm in…" "Okay, then we're driving to Florida tomorrow to see Carlos."

Carlos was another dear friend of ours who had joined the Marines, broken his foot midway through boot camp, and had to stay an additional six months in basic training before being stationed in Pensacola. It was a miserable experience, and he was missing home. Ty drove a thirsty sports car that drank only premium gasoline and got around twelve miles to the gallon. The transmission of my Jeep was ready to fall out, and the only other guy who was willing to join us on such short notice had a small, single cab truck. The truck was a manual, and could only be started by pushing it down the street and popping it into gear. We ended up swapping the sports car for another friend's midsize sedan for the week saying we were going to the coast. Of course, that was interpreted as the Texas coast.

Flashing forward a couple of years to the situation at hand, I called Ty and said, "Hey man, I need to ask you something crazy, but I'm not giving you any details until you give me a yes or no first." He replied with two words made sacred by our friendship,

"I'm in."

"Alright, I need a ride."

"But, you're in Hawaii."

"I just found out my mom has cancer. I'm flying to California. It was the furthest I could get with the money I had. It's a surprise."

"Well then, I'll just have to come pick you up. Be there in two days."

Ty still had the same car though, and he couldn't use mine, because I'd sold it to pay for tuition. It was a good thing the car was nice enough to pull off the old switch-a-roo again. Katherine flew out to meet us, and I got my hands on a video recorder to document the trek home.

We all met in San Francisco at a friend's place. For our last night there, we went to a bar down the street to celebrate the joy of life. Upstairs there was the largest chalkboard I had ever seen; it ran the length of the shotgun-style building. We took turns drawing goofy illustrations, and went line for line writing our own inspiring messages to my mom that played off the last person's words. It ended with the word "survival," followed by the first thing she had ever heard God say to her, "*You don't have a choice.*" Later in the evening I was pulled aside by a gentle hand to read something she had chalked up:

Free Spirit,
You are my soul mate,
Someday we will grow old and,

"Fill in the blank," she whispered to me.
I added: "Sing songs and dance."

It was then signed with love. She and I kissed for the first time that night, and I felt a glimpse of peace in a period of immense uncertainty.

The three of us took a quick glimpse at the Golden Gate, then began driving home for the ultimate surprise for Anna. My hope was to keep her away from the pearly gates before her time. I told no one else of this plan. My companions and I were the only ones who knew. I called my momma and got her voicemail as we were exiting the city. I told her I was in the airport about to board the plane to go to Budapest. I said "Merry Christmas, Happy New Year" and told her that I was rooting for her with love. I then turned off the phone and left it off. We drove many of the same roads I had ridden only six months before. On the last day we drove fourteen straight hours to arrive at 2 a.m. in the small, sleepy town where I had grown up; much too late to unveil myself at home. It was Saturday night. We woke in time to show up unannounced at my father's church. Moments before service began, Ty filmed with the borrowed camera as I snuck in a side door. I was behind my mother while she was walking to her seat. Within earshot, I uttered a single word, "Mom." She stopped dead in her tracks, turned gasping mouth agape, and broke in my arms; thankful that I was obedient to the only place in the world that I needed to be. She was one boob down, and still had a small tube in her chest from the operation she'd had just days before, but she looked more vibrant and alive than ever. I thank God for the people who made that day possible. I thank God that I can still see her shocked expression today on tape. The date was December 23, 2007.

Chapter 8

Winning the Battle

When we hear the word "cancer," we are filled with images. We might envision a commercial set in the children's section of a hospital or a loved one's face. If we're lucky we see a sea of pink circling a track; runners and walkers raising money in a race for the cure. If we're not, we see an assortment of bandanas covering a frail head that has lost its hair. Or worse. The last image I expected to see was that of my mother shimmering and shining for the entire two weeks I still had left at home. It made absolutely no sense. There was no way one could ever look at her and see a disease.

The beginning was the only time I ever saw any apprehension in her. She was adamant about pursuing alternate treatments beside the typical chemotherapy and radiation routes. Within a matter of weeks she had read literature on other treatment methods with comparable or higher success rates of survival that were far less taxing on the body. Chemotherapy is designed to nuke all of the cancer cells. Unfortunately, the blasts are non-discriminatory, and proceed to wreck everything in their wake; including the white blood cells that contribute to a properly working immune system. Anna felt that there were better, documented methods to be tried. And she had the same faith in God that had brought her sister back from certain death.

I've heard of some Christians actually believing they are being punished with disease for their sins, and or that it would go against God's will to treat illness with any method other than prayer. It should be noted that there is a fine line between faith and religious stupidity. There are modern medical practices and vaccines that have tremendously extended life expectancies since the days of widespread plagues. None of those breakthroughs are attributed to a sinful nature, and their use should never be considered against God's will. My mother was not convinced that conventional methods had progressed as far as the medical field claimed, as she saw no difference between her treatment and that provide for her own mother. My father and mother quarreled back and forth until kindly meeting in the middle on traditional and natural forms of treatment. My father's concern was herbal remedies alone, if allowed to become a failed trial, might allow the cancer to spread to the point that traditional treatments would be rendered ineffective later if the cancer had too long to spread. Anna was determined to do things her way, but she also wanted to be responsive to the desires of everyone else in the family that needed her. She said she would be obedient to my father and us, in spite of her own desires. This would be the last time we would have that discussion.

It was February when all of the fun started. I was in a meeting trying to silence the phone in my pocket vibrating against my thigh. It was my father, John. Stepping out to return the call, he informed me that everything had been going really well until my mother had gotten a common cold. It quickly turned into pneumonia when, because of the chemo, she did not have enough white blood cells to fend off the virus. She was in the emergency room. Stuck on a little rock in the middle of the Pacific Ocean, I was trying to remain calm while asking my dad what to do, willing to take the semester off to come home.

- "Are you kidding me? She'll be fine. Stay there. She's just been making a fuss about having to get out of here so she can attend your sister Hilary's powder-puff football game in a few days."

"Where are you guys now?"

"The emergency room."

"And she wants to be out in a few days to go to a football game during the coldest part of the year?"

"She can barely talk, but said there's no way she's missing it."

The doctor reported that a healthy blood count was somewhere between three thousand and five thousand. My mother's had dipped to below four hundred. He said that it would be nearly impossible to get her well enough to be released in time for the game, and out came her Bible. When she finally had enough strength to speak coherently, she called me. Amidst heavy coughing spells, she wanted to tell me about all of the scriptures she was praying on, and how she was going to prove the doctor wrong. "I'm *going* to make that game," she said. It was almost comical to hear such ferocity coming from such a small frame, but she wasn't kidding in the least. Then, it was back to the scriptures. She was cognizant of the numbers and goal at hand, but their distance only made her more determined. The night before game day, the doctor said there was no way her blood count would be high enough by the next afternoon. Unfazed, she called once more to tell me she was believing for a miracle and ready to receive it. To everyone's amazement, she was released an hour before kickoff. They went straight to the stadium. The only visible part of her body not completely wrapped in a mummified state by blankets was everything she needed to see my sister throw several touchdowns in her team's upset over the senior girls. While mom was busy screaming as loud as she could through the heavy covering, the other parents applauded her courage.

The rest of her chemo rounds went without a hitch. With a radical change in diet, her body's good response to the treatments, and an overwhelming amount of support from friends and members in our church, my mom was on a fast track to recovery. When a Susan G. Komen race was scheduled in town, a huge gathering organized to run in support of my momma. They assembled under the team name "Anna's Warriors," a name that came straight from her passionate speeches when asked how she was doing. They even had a big banner and T-shirts made to proudly announce that she was not fighting alone. The two friends that helped me get home for Christmas drove to Waco to step in during my absence. Anna would quickly turn from her mild-tempered sweet demeanor to a fearless warrior for God. She would say repeatedly that she was a warrior, and she didn't have any choice but to fight and survive so she could later spread the message to others struggling with their faith when surrounded by adversity. If you were around her, you'd hear a rally cry that would inspire any soldier in battle.

When I finally made it back home for the summer I was able to help and participate with her. My hair had previously been down to my shoulders after getting comfortable in Hawaii. Recently losing her hair, she had a new 'do when she welcomed me home, and my brother Christian had adopted her new look. Joining in, we had fun busting out the clippers that got clogged several times by the big mop she was trying to shave off of my head. Upon my first visit to her oncologist's office for one of her rounds, the nursing staff was especially welcoming when she came in. They took the liberty of telling me everything they had heard her jibberjabber away about this long-lost son of hers on the other side of the country. They also told me how much they appreciated her presence; she was one of the most selfless patients they had ever treated. No matter how she felt, she would always take time to encourage whoever was in the chair next to her with scripture verses or kind, uplifting words. Once, the nurse said, the roles were reversed—the nurse had a splitting headache no amount of pain relievers had been able to take care of. When my mom heard this, she pulled her aside to pray for her, and she was able to thankfully tell my mother the headache was gone before the round was over. It never stopped with my mom. While she fought for her life, everything she believed and lived on she tried to share with others to brighten their days. Two weeks after I returned to school she didn't have to anymore. Within six months of her diagnosis she had completed treatments and received a clean bill of health. She had beaten cancer and gave all of the glory to God for the victory.

Now that I was able to focus more on graduating, it wasn't as difficult for me to be so far away. My biological father lives out by the lake in Austin. There is a small community of homeowners out there who regularly get together, and a wonderful retired old man from Brooklyn, Mr. Ray. Mr. Ray moved two houses down from my father and quickly became one of our family's greatest friends, constantly asking about how my mother, whom he had never met, was doing. One evening in the fall I had called to say hello to my dad, but Mr. Ray answered his phone for him. We began chatting, and he asked if I would be coming home for Thanksgiving. I explained that I didn't have the time or money to make what usually took around fourteen hours of travel time each way for an extended weekend. He then asked about Christmas. I had just checked the day before, but the cheapest ticket I could find was three hundred seventy-five dollars one-way, and I told him I wouldn't have enough to come home. The next day my dad called me while I was in class. In the voicemail his voice sounded both awkward and serious. He said he had something important to say, but nothing was wrong. As it turns out, Mr. Ray had left a check on his car windshield for the amount of the plane ticket with a note in the memo line stating, "Bring that kid home." Once again, the compassion of friendship was getting me home to my mother for the holidays.

It was wonderful being home without the previous concerns. She was glowing like always, and both of our hair had come back in abundance (except hers returned wavy instead of straight like before). We had a good laugh about the new look and how much trouble she was having trying to learn its quirks in order to style it. Life was good and made even better because she was still with us. After almost a month home, which also included a flourishing relationship with Katherine, who had written her love on the chalkboard the year before, I was going back to Hawaii to finish my final semester. My mom dropped me off at the bus station and I went back to Austin to be with my friends for a few more days. Back at school, I was juggling twenty credit hours, had taken over as president of the largest campus organization (The Wine Toaster's Club), and was actively involved in two other organizations. I was also managing a long-distance romance with words that were quickly manifesting themselves from chalk to reality when she came out to Hawaii to be with me for the last month I was there (between the middle of April and May). If I didn't already have enough on my plate, the phone call I received in early February definitely tipped the fragile balance.

While trying to enjoy some downtime before the busy upcoming week, I was out surfing and hanging with friends at the beach when my parents called. Once again, they seemed nonchalant enough to not draw any suspicion, but they then informed me that the cancer had come back in my mother; this time in her liver and patches on her lungs. The news was devastating, but there she was again chastising my concerns. "Tyler, I beat it once, and I'll be it again. This is an attack on my life trying to prevent me from spreading God's word, but I *will* live because God can't use me from the grave. We *will* win." There was no point in addressing any doubts because she didn't possess any, and she had no need for that type of conversation. The only thing to do was to get on board and be inspired by her spirit.

Some people are naturally optimistic and in circumstances like the one my mother was in, it can be tough to get a straightforward answer from them. It did no good to try to search for a second opinion from my father. Her greatest asset was the fact that with his pastoral position, he was allowed to accompany her to every appointment and chemo round—he was essentially there for her every waking moment. When I would ask him how things were really going, he would reinforce that her optimism was not just a partial show; it was the most consistent spectacle of genuine courage he had ever seen. He made it clear that even in private conversations alone at night, she never once showed any fear or spoke about the idea of dying, and her faith was more solid than any stone the devil might try to mark her resting place with. There were days when she sounded great on the phone, and there were days that really scared me, but she never deviated away from the consistency of her message, and we all stood rooting with her.

The problem with this second round of efforts, as opposed to the first, was that one's body needs a fully functioning liver to process all of the toxins from the chemo. When the liver is also under attack, your body gets stuck in a catch-22—the body becomes too toxic to handle the heavy rounds of treatment, but also needs the heavy rounds to keep the cancer from spreading. Without any real way of gauging the dosage levels, and their possible outcomes, Anna struggled with an experimental treatment phase that often took a heavy toll on her physical strength without having any effect on her mental strength.

In what appeared to be her weakest state, my mother became more determined than ever. Two years before, when I decided to go to school in Hawaii, there was no way for me to have known how seemingly impossible it would be for her to see me graduate. (If anything, I thought I was doing them a favor by setting up an obligated dual-purpose getaway to a tropical island.) Now my mother was strongly encouraged by her doctor not to make the trip in her condition, especially since she was starting a new treatment, which began with the administration of the highest doses, right before they were set to leave. Even worse, she was breathing on an oxygen tank at the time, and they wouldn't be able to have the tank on the plane because of the altitude pressure. My dad, John, went out of his way to work out the kinks so she would have what she needed. He said he didn't have a choice, because she was determined to go to Hawaii if it was the last thing she ever did. Much later I learned that she'd had a terrible coughing fit on the plane, and almost didn't make it when she couldn't breathe for an extended period of time. Nevertheless, my parents, a dear friend from Florida, and my girlfriend who had come to be with me for the last month out there, had all made it out for the joyous event. Momma didn't do well with warm weather, and had to stay in the hotel most of the time. This was not a problem, as they were on the twelfth floor and had an ocean view right across from the beach. She still made it out for dinner and down to the sand to watch me surf. We enjoyed a sunset together, and I was ecstatic to have her there getting to participate in my life the way she loved to do.

On the big day, I knew it would be tricky to organize everything for her. She was still on some serious painkillers that would knock her out if she didn't time them correctly. There was no way my parents were going to be able to attend the ceremony in its entirety, but with the traffic and parking challenges, there would also be no way to get them in and out quickly. Fortunately, my friend from Florida had also lived in Hawaii, and offered to chauffeur my parents. Another friend, who lived right behind the arena, graciously gave up his parking spot so my friend could park there. The graduates were essentially allowed to sit anywhere they wanted, and I sat as far back as I could to give them enough time to get into the building.

When I texted my father to let him know it had all begun, he replied that my mother didn't feel well and probably wouldn't make it. I was completely crushed. Despite the filled seats, in which I could see a group of loyal supporters holding signs with my name, and some of them already getting kicked out of their spots; pushed further back after being too obnoxious directly behind the ceremony leader, I felt a huge void. It wasn't so much self-pity, as it was the responsibility of "forcing" my mom to come as far as she had—only to leave her with the burdens of a potential belief that she'd hurt my feelings. When those in the row in front of me stood up, I sent one last text to my father to let him know I was about to walk. I promptly received the response, "Great, we're right behind you." As it turned out, the parking spot I had gotten them was on the back side of the arena at the bottom of the downward slope it was built on. Without knowing where they were or where to enter, they wheeled her in through the same doors as the processional, instead of the upper level where the general entrances are, and security let them pass. My mother was on the floor in the center aisle as I walked down from the stage in cap and gown. I was the only student in the whole house who got to embrace his mother immediately after receiving his diploma. I wish you could've seen her face, but there are just some things that will forever remain solely mine, and that look is one of them.

Shortly thereafter everyone left. I had one week to wrap things up in Hawaii before heading back to Texas. From there I was going to South America, where I was going to finish up school studying Spanish and obtain my remaining six credits. My girlfriend picked me up at the airport in San Antonio to spend the day with her family. We then had one night with our friends in Austin, one day with my biological father at the lake, and a day and a half at my parents' home in Waco before heading to Dallas to fly out. It was a whirlwind trip that left me spinning when my father, John, called me on our way to Waco to tell me my mother had just checked into the intensive care unit at the hospital. When she had gotten home the treatment left her so weak that she was unable to eat. She became so frail they had to admit her so as to get the necessary fluids and sustenance pumped back into her body to survive. I was scheduled to be out of the country for two months, and only had one night to decide whether to go. My dad made it seem as though it was an easy choice. "Go," he said, "we'll be fine. You need to finish up. We won't have you quitting now or taking time off. Get on the plane. We'll still be here when you get back."

His confidence didn't make the decision any easier. Ultimately though, to have stayed would have been to acknowledging what I saw over our faith, and when she came to I didn't want to have to explain that I stayed behind thinking she wasn't going to make it. In order to complete my degree, my final classes had to be taken through the school, with the exception of the study abroad program I was participating in. If I didn't go, I would have had to go back to Hawaii for at least another semester, and I didn't want to be that far away for so long. With a heavy heart I said good-bye to my mom without the ability of a response from her, and my girlfriend drove me to Dallas to get on a plane for Argentina. She was headed up to Montana to work on a lodge while I was gone, and we had plans to meet back up when I returned stateside.

If you thought you could count Anna out now, you obviously haven't been paying attention. While she spent almost a month in the hospital, there was still more to be seen by her. You see, my sister Hilary also had a graduation to attend—high school. My mother called me about a week after I had gotten settled into my home in Mendoza, Argentina, to say she was sorry for not saying good-bye. I couldn't believe how great she sounded on the phone, and she laughed with me saying, "I know. I'm getting better every day!" The big joke (again) was on her doctor, who had become all too familiar with her refusal to follow his recommendation that she remain in the hospital when he didn't see it fit to release her. Had it been anyone else, he said he would have never released someone in her state, but after twenty-four days in the hospital; he knew he had to do everything he could to get my mom ready to fly the coup. On the day of Hilary's graduation, she was up to fifty pounds over her normal weight, unable to adequately release excess fluids. Significantly bloated and fragile, she left the hospital early to be in attendance of every picture and moment of another one of her baby's big days. Thank God there were no other major events going on. There's no telling what lengths she would have submitted herself to.

I had toured the wine country in Argentina, surfed the frigid waters of the Pacific during the Southern Hemisphere's winter on the coast of Chile, traversed the salt flats of the Bolivian desert, bicycled down the world's most dangerous road, trekked through the Peruvian jungle up to Machu Picchu, and still couldn't wait to be home. There was nothing I wanted more.

Chapter 9

A Life of Impact

It took more than two and one-half days on buses and several airport layovers to finally make it back stateside. Fortunately, I flew into Houston late in the night. After turning my phone on for the first time in months, I was trying to arrange a ride with a friend or a taxi to take me to my grandparents' house, only to find a whole crew of family waiting for me at the airport. After my mom had recovered from her nearly one month stint in the hospital, she had a terrible feeling about the medication she was being given, and asked for a second opinion. My grandpa, John's father, is a well-respected doctor in Houston, and immediately had her scheduled for appointments in the world-class facility at MD Anderson Cancer Center.

It seemed as if everything was swirling full circle for me. When I was raising money for the Texas 4000, our team was given the opportunity to choose specifically where our money would go. We opted to donate to one research project, and give the other portion to the building of a hope lodge at MD Anderson for parents who came from out of town to be with their afflicted children. With the addition of this wing, the parents could stay right across the street for free throughout the duration of their children's treatments. I could still see those kids' faces, and how happy they were just to have someone there playing with them. I remember the gratitude of the parents, for someone who cared enough to offer them hope while they waited patiently for better days.

Now it was my family that needed reassuring news. It was close to one in the morning when I made it to my grandparents' house where my family was staying. My dad was smiling at the front door. He said Momma had been up the whole time waiting to say hello; she would rest easier knowing I was home. In the morning they were to get the results on some tests that had been run. Initially, my parents were told that my mother would most likely be staying in Houston to receive treatment for at least two months. We were all eagerly waiting in the living room when she got home from the appointment. There was good news and bad news. The good news was that she'd been justified in her request for a second opinion. Her liver could not handle any of the medications she was prescribed before, and she would have died had she taken them. The latter news was there was no treatment that could bypass the necessary functions of the liver. The prognosis at this point was the best remedies now would be for her to enjoy her time at home and prayer. She just laughed telling me about how she amazed the doctor with her ability to walk around a bit and travel back and forth between Waco and Houston.

One of our uncles works for an airline, and has family in Belgium. We stayed long enough in Houston to see my brother Christian off for a spontaneous trip to Europe, and headed back to Waco. Little Rachel had remained faithfully at home for the entire summer, and had been invited by one of her best friends to go on a two-week vacation to Florida. The two girls remind me of my mother and her best friend from the old, faded photos that I've seen of them. Rachel's mannerisms and innocence are synonymously picturesque with my mother's younger version. Dad said that while Rachel was having a blast, she called home every time she got a chance, and also just wanted to be home. Rachel is the sweet one in the family. With Christian and Rachel out of town, Hilary and I were the only kids at the house in Waco. Happy to be back in the car and on her way home, Momma was unscathed by the whole event. She was the one encouraging us to enjoy every fun occasion that presented itself.

When we got back to the house, it was refreshing to see all of the scripture verses specific to courage and healing that were written in her elegant handwriting and posted on every mirror and frequently passed wall. Sporadically throughout each day I saw the supplemental source of her strength in the form of our church members. There was a small window of time each day when my mom was awake and feeling good enough to be out in the living room. While that window was open, so were our doors, and people came and went constantly. Lunch would be brought by one person and dinner by another. Someone else came to pick up our laundry, while a whole team of ladies came for over an hour for prayer. The prayer was direct and intense. I could see why my mother called the group Anna's Warriors. Each one of those women possessed extraordinary strength, able to lift a car off a child if need be, like you hear on the news. For that hour of prayer, I would not have wanted to take on a single one of them in their spiritual battle. At night, after my mom had gone to bed, I would go out to see old friends in town. No matter what time I returned there was always a dark gray Cadillac with tinted windows parked out front. It scared me at first, looking like some sort of scene from a mob movie, but in the car sat a woman praying through the entire night for my mom's life. This devotion wasn't in response to the latest prognosis, it was something that took place consistently, each and every day. These were true acts of faith. I was blown away by the faithful diligence of these champions.

With education comes a certain cynicism. In school, I had studied many accounts of empirical nations using missionaries to cast the natives' ways or dress as evil. They destroyed local customs and practices, all with the alternative aspiration of taking their lands and enslaving the people in the name of conversion (more than I cared to hear). It happened all over the Pacific. It happened all over our country with the Native Americans. It's happened all over the world. On top of religion's historical background, it often feels that the church is constantly in the hot seat for the scandals of its leaders today.

I admit, at times, it was difficult to witness this blatant abuse of God's intentions and not lose faith in the church, until I came home. It is the nature of the news to report only that which demands headlines. For a sanctity which has always promoted the betterment of humanity, it is only when people deviate away from these progressive values that the world gets access to the deeds of the wrong people in the form of poor publicity representing the church as a whole. I was rejuvenated by the efforts of the church's genuine members, and unseen families across the country, who surrounded us. They organized on Sundays, and they organized around my mother. They effectively reshaped my faith with their sincere generosity and devoted willingness to see one of their own all the way to the promised lands of healing outlined in the Bible for its believers. It blesses my heart to know it is still happening all over the world by good people who never make the news.

The date was August 5, 2009. Rachel was coming back into town from Florida. Christian was also scheduled to return from Europe later in the evening. My sister Hilary and I had the privilege to hang out alone for a few days with Mom and Dad before she left for the University of Arkansas, but she had left that morning to go to a friend's lake house with their family outside of Dallas. Mom was getting placed in the care of hospice that morning, and Dad and I were waiting in a quiet home for the workers to show for an instructive meeting. Mom didn't feel well, and she told my dad she wanted to stay in bed and rest. It was to be one of the last things she would have the strength to say before going virtually incapacitated the rest of the day.

When I returned from South America, Momma had a list of books that she wanted me to read. It was all of the literature she had stood steady on, and one of the first books I opened (it was actually more of a pamphlet on healing) was by Dodie Osteen. My mom loved to tell me the story about receiving a call from Mrs. Osteen one day while she was in the hospital, and how stern Dodie was with her. Dodie had explained that there was no time or room for her to feel sorry for herself, so she'd just have to believe in God's healing and get up. In this book, one of the first passages spoke of Mrs. Osteen's diagnosis with liver cancer (like my mom), and how because of the disease's destructive nature she was given only two weeks to live. I almost couldn't believe it when I read that, as though it was common knowledge. I had never done any research about liver cancer because Momma said she was going to beat whatever she faced, and damn it, I believed her. I thought about how she had made it long past two weeks (and multiple graduations). I thought about her first miracle when she made it to Hilary's powder puff football game. Momma later found out the husband of a family we knew had gotten pneumonia around the same time and wasn't even fighting cancer. He was physically fit and training for a triathlon, but had died within a matter of days. My mother, in contrast, was not much more than one hundred pounds of sheer determination. She had already made it through so much. She proved the human will is something to never be underestimated.

The hospice physicians finally showed up. I listened from a small room nearby as they told my dad in the living area she had a few days at most, based on the reactions of her body. Afterward, he told me that the doctors in Houston had told them the cancer had spread to her brain. They decided not to tell us in order to keep our spirits on a par with hers. He said she refused to give up even when she was told to just go home.

Similar to the last night with Uncle Bill, everyone quickly scrambled to make it into town. Rachel made it back first. Hilary had just arrived at the lake when she got the call to turn around, which her friend's mother immediately did. One of my mom's best friends, whom they'd shared many days painting and decorating their homes at the husbands' expenses, made it into town passing through on a well-timed trip. Her sisters and father, Aunt Junie, Aunt Chris, and Papa Al, all traveled from San Antonio, Bandera, and Austin. And as for me, well, for the first time I was right where I needed to be. We were all right where we needed to be, with her.

Anna was responsive to stimuli. She would try to kick the covers off her legs when we covered her up, and she would squeeze our hands when we told her we loved her, but she was unable to verbally communicate, and was taking long hard breaths for gulps of air. I remember this rhythmic breathing pattern from the last time I saw Uncle Bill. I remembered seeing Papa Al sobbing in the corner over the loss of his son, and the memories of grown men's tears have haunted me since. I feared the possibility of having to see them again for another one of his children. Hilary and I spoke candidly about a mutual sentiment of being caught off guard. Mom had sold us on the concept of one product: survival. We bought it, cherished the idea, and never let it depreciate in value. Now, there we were being told that we needed to say good-bye, which contradicted everything that had sustained us for the last two years. We weren't ready to accept it. We hadn't prepared for this outcome, ever.

Hilary was upset over the notion that there was still too much she wanted our mother to be here to see. "What about my college graduation, and my wedding. God I just want her be there when I walk down the aisle. Tyler, do you think she'll be able to see us?" I didn't have an answer for her. I was still trying to process everything myself. She went on to tell me about when she was saying good-bye, Mom had snapped out of her condition to tell her to stop crying. Everything she said was indicative of the story my mom had told me about Uncle Bill becoming lucid long enough to say he was holy, and have it validated, before he lost his awareness again. Hilary kept repeating, "She looked up at me right in the eyes and said, 'Hilary, stop crying. Everything is going to be okay. Everything is going to be okay. I'll find a way to talk to you.' It was crazy. I didn't have a choice but to try to stop crying."

Christian was the last one to make it in. He had flown to Europe on standby tickets, and had to fly home the same way. He had been stuck there for a few days when he was informed he needed to do everything he could to get on the next flight before it was too late. Immediately after landing in Houston, Aunt Donna rushed him the additional three hours back to Waco. Throughout the day, Dad had been telling Mom that he was coming and to hold on for him. It was after midnight when he finally arrived. Christian went to the back to talk to our mother once more. It was tough on him to see her unable to respond to him. Trying to make sure she knew he loved her, he said to her, "Mom, did you hear me?" Still kneeling at the edge of her bed, Mom made an extra effort to reach a quivering arm up and put her hand on Christian's shoulder to acknowledge his love before it fell back to her side.

I remember being relieved when everyone had finally stopped shuffling in and out of her room, and we were all ablc to be quiet and go to bed. I felt near a point of exhaustion from all of the emotions and commotions of the day. I finally lay down and fell asleep in the back room on the other side of the house around one in the morning. Dad had turned the lights off, but stayed awake counting her respirations. They were regular, between eighteen and twenty per minute, when he began to pray for her life. He spoke to the Lord and asked Him not to prolong the suffering any further, if our prayers were not going to be answered the way we had wished. While he was still praying he noticed he could no longer hear her breathing. Dad quickly jumped up to turn the bedside light on. Nearly twenty years before he had taken her hands into his own and pledged to love and stay by her side; to have and to hold her, in sickness and health, until death would they part. He was now holding her hands in much the same way, having honored and loyally fulfilled his promise to her. It is said many people will hold on for days, afraid to depart from the world leaving grudges and unresolved issues looming behind after they're gone. My mom had neither of these. Dad leaned in and whispered in her ear, "Honey, it's okay. I love you and release you. Go be with the Lord." At his request she took one more peaceful breath.

At 1:43 a.m., the door opened. It was my dad. He said, "Tyler, you need to wake up. Your mother just left to go be in heaven." I remember sitting in a surreal silence in the darkness of the room trying to comprehend falling asleep with a mother in this world, and waking up without one. I was paralyzed by the irreversible finality of this thought. Throughout the house, lights were turning on. Some family members were staying at a neighbor's across the street, and I heard their front door open. I heard Hilary, almost hysterical, repeatedly praising Momma's new existence in a better place. I heard Christian fighting with her to stop, unwilling to see the glory in that yet. I remember all of this and not knowing what the hell to do.

I remember the last things I said to her, and although I am more than willing to share much of my time with her, there will always be things that will stay just with me. I remember wanting to run, wanting to get away, wanting it all to just disappear when I woke up from what must have been a terrible dream. There was no way to prepare for what I saw next. Everyone had gathered in various locations in the house, but I didn't want to be near anyone. I put my head down and went straight for the front door to go outside and be alone in the night. When I looked up, however, our street was already filled with people. There was an entire congregation of cars and patrons blockading the entrance of our neighborhood with their presence. It was a truly unbelievable sight. I must have been in literal shock or something. When I came to, I noticed my dad was already out there preaching to them like our yard was his Sunday pulpit. He was still proclaiming her faith, that she had refused to give up, and the fight was not over with her physical death when her spirit was still eternally alive in heaven. He pleaded with the crowd to go home, but no one budged. They stood and clapped, and continued to pray. I was in awe of her impact. You see such reverence when we lose the likes of the Kennedys and Dr. King. It seemed she had earned a spot right between Mother Teresa and the Father, entering the gates of heaven as a queen. It was August 6, 2009; a night I'll never forget. Anna Rambeau was forty-four years old.

Chapter 10

Hoping to Cope

By the time the morning sun had risen, the news had quickly traveled. More friends and family had arrived, and the house was buzzing with countless others bringing cards and food. I went into a weird mental state. There was too much noise, too many people, and not enough time to be alone with my thoughts. I didn't want anybody to tell me they were so sorry for my loss. I didn't want anybody's pity. I just wanted to shut off and let it all go away. I was too scared to show any emotion, not wanting to draw any extra attention to myself out of fear of even more hands or hugs all over me. My family and girlfriend were there, and that was enough to keep me going. I was numb to anyone other than them.

There is about a week missing from my life's recollection that can only be revisited by quick flashes in time. Other than those flashes, not much remains. A year later I began to realize the lapse of memory, particularly when I would see old friends who'd been there at the time. While visiting a friend in the hospital, one lady in particular kept telling everyone in the room how great my songs were; she went on and on about my music. I got confused, thinking it had been many years since I had last seen her, long before I even started playing the guitar. I finally asked what song she was talking about, and she said, “The song! You know; the song you sang at your mother’s service!” The sanctuary was packed the day we laid my mother to rest. Christian and I got up on stage to play a song I had written for her. He played piano, and I played guitar and sang. I remember seeing the spotlight, and standing in front as a family after the service was over, but don’t remember who came by, or who said what.

The only comfort was the stories that were revealed. Dad told me that the second time the cancer struck, they had found out while I was still home. They waited until I was comfortably back in Hawaii to tell me, because the only thing Anna wanted was for me to finish school. He told me they developed a policy of informing without intruding into our normal routines. No matter how terrible she felt, she would get up every morning to take the kids to school, and she picked them up to bring them home. She still made dinner almost every night and didn't want to alter her family's lifestyles one bit, attempting not to alter anyone's spirits. I tried to think about how she acted when we said good-bye, if there was any indication of fear that it might be our last parting in person when she let me go. We were rushing to get me to a bus station. I hadn't eaten lunch. I ran in to grab a ticket while she tried to find some food for me before the bus pulled out. She got me a sandwich. It was a cold, dreary day. She waited in the car waving until I was out of sight. She smiled the entire time. There was no sign of fear. Dad said there were Sunday mornings when she felt horrible. He would strongly urge her to stay in bed and rest, but she would crawl to her closet and point at the outfit she wanted to wear. She told him the enemy could not relish in any victories on her account. We laughed in disbelief of her courage. We cried that it was not rewarded the way we had asked for.

When it was all over, and she was gone, I went to spend the weekend with friends in Austin. One night I had a dream. I've always had vivid, colorful dreams with memorable details, but this was unlike any other. It began badly. I was riding along in some kind of police chase. There were sirens and tires squealing around turns, with dirt and gravel getting kicked up against the car doors. The images had the pixilation of an old film reel with recently incorporated color technology. Just then the car being chased flipped sliding upside down on the pavement. The support frames had collapsed from the impact and there was shattered glass all over the ground mixed with the blood of the driver and the terrifying screams of the passenger.

To edit old films, they would cut the strips and superimpose another together in the right order. It felt like that happened with my dream. With a smooth, instantaneous transition I was in another dream scene.

It was my parents' bedroom, but rearranged and redecorated. The colors were shimmering, almost glowing from the vivacious light shining through the windows, and there she was leaning up against the side of the bed. It was my mom. She was wearing blue jeans and a tattered pink polo shirt splattered with blotches of white paint; the shirt she always wore when she was decorating. She was in the healthy form I always knew her as, not the lifeless deflated shell she became. Her hair was back, and she was smiling from ear to ear. The smile was a blend of ecstatic joy and a satisfied, overcome-all-odds look of defiance. She was stunningly gorgeous.

Despite everything in front of me I was still conscious it was a dream, and was further cognizant of her passing the week before. Without knowing what to do I just said,

"Mom?"

"Tyler." It was her voice, with the same subtle spike in tone on the *y*.

"Mom, what are you doing here?"

"See, I told you I'd find a way to talk to you!"

I realized this related to my conversation with Hilary, and the questions she had asked.

"Oh, okay. Well, can you see us?"

"Of course! It's great, I can see everything! I can see your greatest accomplishments and even what you're looking at on the Internet."

She realized the last statement had caught me off guard.

"I'm just messing with you," she said, "but seriously, I can see everything. It's wonderful."

That was her humor. I knew it was her. I was elated that this was somehow more than a dream, and ran to her. Right before our embrace I started doubting again. "Is this some kind of hologram that will flicker as my hands pass through nothing?" I thought. It was too late. I was already there going for it. Instead of a ghost, my arms clasped naturally around her back, and I could literally feel her being. In astonishment I said, "Mom, I can feel you!"

"I know. That's because I'm real." We held each other for a minute until she looked up at me. "Listen honey, I've gotta go now."

Breaking into tears, I tried to hold on longer. "No, Mom, I'm not ready yet. I'm not ready yet!"

"Hey, what I did tell you guys? Everything's going to be alright…"

With the same seamless cut, I was back in the original dream with the glass, blood, and screaming. I couldn't take anymore and woke myself up. Lying in my bed, in the darkness, I wept the rest of the night. For the next few days I must've played those events over countless times; analyzing her smile, her mannerisms, and her words. Each time I didn't get far before breaking down into tears. Finally, I was able to grab hold of the most powerful thing she had said with respect to my being able to physically feel her in a dream state, "I know, that's because I'm *real.*" It became so reassuring—she had not only answered the questions that drive people crazy for years on end, but had also authenticated her ongoing existence.

I'd been home for barely a month when I got the call. It was one of my closest friends and roommate from Hawaii, Jordan. Jordan had also graduated, with a degree in engineering, and was home in Florida with a proposition. He had an old '83 VW Vanagon Bus needing to be where it belonged, on open roads. I packed a bag, my guitar, and booked a ticket out there. My girlfriend even came along to Florida for a few days to see me off. We were to be traveling for at least two months, or until we ran out of money; whichever came first. In the end it was neither. We blew the engine in the first week while cruising through South Carolina. Thankfully we were visiting family at the time. They put us up and arranged for us to do some construction work, buying us time to figure out our next move. I was in no hurry to go home. I didn't know it yet, but I was running. It was so pretty there that we decided to stay and live in Charleston. We used the construction money toward an awesome house we found downtown. My girlfriend said she couldn't wait for me to return to Texas, so she loaded up her car and joined us; quickly finding her own place and job.

As far as the pain was concerned, I was used to being half way across the country for the months that made up a typical semester. My girlfriend was worried I was bottling too much up, but the loss wasn't something I was ready to deal with. I had what I needed: a job that kept me busy, great friends, a warm heart to hold onto each night when I got home, beautiful new surroundings, and a beach with decent surf. Come Thanksgiving my girlfriend was getting homesick. She comes from a large, wonderful family, and she wasn't accustomed to spending extended amounts of time away from them. I had her running all over the country for me. She wanted to go home, and I didn't want to stop her. She petitioned with me to come home with her, but I wasn't ready. Moreover, in Texas we'd be living thirty miles apart from each other, and I didn't have a car. It's impossible to get around Texas without a car. I told her everything would work out. It did and it didn't.

My biological father had been driving his vehicle for eight years. It was time for a new one. He said the trade-in value was miniscule in comparison to having me home and called to barter, saying I could have his old car if I came back. Jordan finally got an engineering job back in Hawaii (after hunting for a year), and we filled the house with new tenants in less than a week so we could both leave. My stepsisters were going to school a little more than an hour away at the University of South Carolina, and were driving to Texas to spend Christmas with their mom and my dad. I hitched a ride up to the school to drive back with them. Everything was falling into place when my girlfriend and I broke up before I could make it back to Texas in time. It seemed the stress of being apart, the instability of our lives, and the neverending emotional roller coaster had rattled our hearts a few too many times.

We drove straight through the night to get out to the lake. I spent one entire day out there, and then made it back to Waco in time to pack a bag and drive to Colorado for Christmas. John didn't want to spend Christmas at home without Mom. It was apparent why. The second I walked in the door I felt a complete loss of life. The walls didn't have the same color. The halls seemed empty. It was quiet and drab. I couldn't believe how different the house felt without her, and it all hit me at once. That moment I was slapped in the face by the reality that she was gone. These were the times I was used to spending with her after long stints away, but I could no longer run from the truth. There was nowhere to hide now.

Ty lived alone in a two-bedroom apartment twenty miles north of Austin. He had been my best friend since we were kids, and was quick to open his door to me upon my return. I had done a clinical research study and made enough money to get by comfortably for a few months, which was good, because the next few months were the hardest of my entire life. I went into a depression and a darkness I didn't know was possible for me. I had always been a happy, confident guy. That was all stripped. I lost fifteen pounds from constant anxiety, and I had difficulty sleeping at night. There were only two things that could put me to bed: either crying for my mother until reaching a point of exhaustion, or a few glasses of straight whiskey. Even friends I wasn't very close to asked me not to drink. Okay. I didn't have a problem with alcohol, but I'd easily be awake until 4 or 5 a.m., unable to calm the nerves, and up again at 7 or 8 a.m. The trauma from the breakup with my girlfriend didn't help.

I'd known the discomfort of heartbreak before, but my mother was the only person I could comfortably go to with matters of the heart. She was a brilliant listener and always knew exactly what to say to set my soul at peace. She could level you with the most eloquent insight you never knew she possessed. And of course, she had a sweet motherly voice and motherly hugs that made the burning of every cut and scratch go away. I wanted to run to my mom now, and my desire for her comfort only reinforced the fact I could not go to her. There is no pain like the loss of a woman, and I had lost the two most important women in my life. It was almost too much to bear.

In the mornings when I woke up alone, I could not even find the motivation to get out of bed. I rarely left the house, except to get groceries. I didn't even tell any of my friends I was back in Austin, knowing I wasn't fit to be in social settings. I had forgotten how to smile. The first time I was around a group of friends, we were watching the Super Bowl.

A commercial came on advertising some antidepressant prescription. As they rattled off the symptoms of depression, I listened in unexpressive disgrace knowing I had and was trying to hide every one of them.

The most tormenting feelings came from not being able to see my mom enjoy her health in the last months. Being sick for a few days straight gets incredibly frustrating. I can't imagine being sick for months and years; not having the strength to run around outdoors or to do any of the things we take for granted in our normal course of action. I hate that she endured so much for herself and for us and did not reap the benefits of her struggle. It broke my heart to have to push her in a wheelchair when she should have been up running and jumping with vitality, praising her healing.

Everyone seemed to need to give his input as to how I could best get my life back together, but I would just affirmatively nod and pretend to appreciate the feeble advice. I was sure that they had no clue about my feelings. Aside from time to heal, what I really needed was to go home. Sure, I was back in the places where I had grown up, but I had not taken the time to go home to the Father. I tried an Internet search for local nondenominational churches. With location and home page substance as factors, I made a metaphorical "blind spin" through my findings with an outstretched finger until randomly choosing whichever was being pointed at when the spin stopped. I went there. Have you ever gotten the suspicion that a certain Sunday message was tailored exactly to your needs? Well, either this was the case that morning, or I was so screwed up *any* message would have been applicable. Nevertheless, it felt good to have made the trip. I was excited to be able to call my dad and tell him the news. I often wonder if I was the kid for whom parents pray to willingly go back to God on his own, without being forced. My parents did such a great job raising me and never asked for any recognition. They never gave way to the pressures of trying to be cool or attempting to be my friend when they needed to be diligent in their roles as parents and as authority figures. Now that I see what they went through to be there for me, I like to tell them as often as possible that they did well and that I have respectfully taken their teachings to heart.

I waited until John was done preaching his own service to call. He got fired up and said, "Ah man, you need to go to Gateway Church. A buddy I grew up with pastors there. He's got a great thing going on down there." It was funny. This was in fact the place I had randomly chosen. John asked me to say hello to his friend on my next visit. When I approached the pastor at the next opportunity, he was warm and gave me his contact information so he could plug me in with a fitting small group. I welcomed this notion since I was attending services alone and because of the enormous crowds he was attracting each week.

It was a Tuesday afternoon when I received an e-mail from a guy inviting me to a college small group he was heading up. It was great, and while he definitely had the attention of his students, the subject matter wasn't quite what I was looking for. Afterward, he said a bunch of the leaders from surrounding churches got together for their own small fellowship at a local pub, and I was welcome to come if I wanted to grab a couple of beers with them the following night. Alright, this is my kind of small group, I thought! There I got wrapped in conversation with another man who was searching, unabashedly, for his faith. He invited me to another group the next night, and I accepted. Mostly I wanted an excuse to get out of the house, but I also was curious about who I might meet next.

The structure of this night struck a sweet melodic chord with my spirit. Everyone joined together, sang, and each member spoke about the topic he was studying. The crowd was attentive and engaged, and then it broke into men's and women's groups for open forums. I stayed relatively quiet, taking comfort in not having to front any false pretenses with the guys in the group. I felt so much pressure to act as "normal" as possible with people who I knew. When I wasn't the same fun-loving guy they remembered me as, they invariably started probing about my emotional state.

It's impossible to explain the huge void left from a parent's loss. I didn't know how to tell people I felt completely lost; that my most knowledgeable historian was gone and took all of her research with her. She knew the exact time all of her children were born, and our lengths and weights to the ounce. She knew every one of our social security numbers off the top of her head. She saw each of our personalities and quirky mannerisms take shape, and the root causes of the inner mechanisms that made us tick. She knew stories that no one else did, our favorite foods, and all of our ticklish spots when we needed to be cheered up. She had the mother's intuition that busted me every time I tried to do something I wasn't supposed to, as well as the exact moments to step in to guard me from harm. She was my greatest source of encouragement and confidence. These were the things that made her *my* mother, rendering no one else qualified for the recently open position. There was no way for me to explain that although I was considered a man, I felt reduced to the longing of a child. I felt like a kid alone on a playground, begging for attention, to be pushed on the swing, or to be proudly told I was doing it correctly on my own. There was no way to explain to anyone that while I used to (seemingly, anyway) have everything figured out, now nothing made sense. Frankly, I didn't want to talk about it anyway, but these guys didn't know me. For all they knew, I really was just a strange quiet dude. It was refreshing to not feel the need to explain anything to them until I was ready.

Chapter 11

Tying it All Together

My recollection escapes me regarding how the exact details unfolded, but we were sitting outside under the moon on a chilly evening in the period when the guys and girls would break into separate groups. Someone was speaking of a personal matter that he was dealing with. He was not alone, which I knew from hearing of similar incidences related by others in the group. My mother's story was relevant somehow to the discussion, and I finally shared parts of it. As I spoke I kept my head down and addressed the men slowly, trying to keep my composure. So much effort was put into keeping it together emotionally. This was an all-time low for me. As a man, it was the weakest I had ever felt. The weakness seemed debilitating to a point where I had neglected to speak until that moment, believing I had nothing to offer anyone else before.

To my astonishment, when I looked up most of the men sitting at the table had not made the same self-conscious efforts I had to withhold the effect that my mother's life had on them. Tears were streaming from the faces of men who had never known her except through my accounts of who she was and what she stood for. The impression left on them instigated a major transition in thought for me. Most people can't associate with the things I used to draw strength from. Most people can't associate with riding a bicycle more than four thousand miles in one summer, moving to an island where they had no friends and no place to live, or traveling alone on buses through multiple third-world countries. However, everyone can associate with loss and pain. Whatever form that loss comes in, even if it doesn't include the severity of a loved one so close as a mother, it is still felt in a way that can bring even the strongest to his knees. No, instead it was the unreserved truth of my weakness that was the most I had to offer to others. This was my reconnection to humanity; to those suffering and struggling like me.

These were great strides for me at the time, but still not enough to suppress the overwhelming amount of weight strapped to my soul and still hindering the forward steps of my journey. The days making up the majority of the week were much too lonely to handle. I thought about how much more difficult my life had become since she left. I thought about how easy my life used to seem. I never used to stress or become demoralized quickly, now I was drowning in anxiety and discouragement. I thought about when I was happiest. I remembered when my biggest problem was that I could never seem to keep the sand out of my hair or bed (coincidentally this was also the least of my worries). I missed being outside, surrounded by God's wonderful creations. On good days we would go surfing. On bad days we would go surfing. On the barefoot walk home, everything was always better. That was it. I was sick of the stronghold this depression had on my life. I was sick of the late-night text messages I would get from my ex saying she missed me, and her inability to support that sentiment the next day when I asked for her to expand on what she wanted from me. I was sick of what seemed like malicious plays on my vulnerability and no longer having the defenses to guard my heart.

I packed my surfboard, a sleeping bag, and my Bible; turned off my phone and headed for the ocean. I was just happy to be back on open roads again with music and pleasant weather, but I should have taken the time to check the forecast. The constant shift in Texas terrain is so invigorating. My hand flowed freely out the window as cities turned into countryside, flatlands turned into rolling hills, and as golden grass gave way to old oaks on the side of the road; all on the way to the coast. Yes, this is what I had been missing.

It was late when I finally arrived. I stopped at a grocery store for firewood and supplies, all while a terrible storm began to blow in. By the time I came out the wind was bitter and biting at the exposed parts of my fingers and face. At the beach there was nothing blocking me from the cold blowing straight off the water onto every portion of my campsite. It was unbearable. There was no way I'd be able to stay there. I drove back to where the buildings were to park up against something that could shield me from the wind so I had a chance of sleeping. It was then that I pulled out my Bible.

I don't think I'm in uncommon company to say one of the essential setbacks to my faith is realistic reasoning. I was the disciple needing to see and touch the holes in Jesus's hands to believe he had risen from the grave. I had distanced myself from God for so long that I had completely forgotten what His presence felt like. Now, the fellowship and

Sunday morning messages were great, but I still didn't have this promise of having the holes in my heart filled up with His love as the preachers kept speaking about. Oh, how lost I was. I'd grown up in the church my entire life, and yet was an absolute amateur to the needs of a relationship which was once so developed.

The reality was that there was a silenced voice deep within me screaming to be released. There are times I feel more than helpless, where my insides want to burst open for not having any way of seeing my mother once more. I could almost literally dive in derangement across the room, over and over, hoping to grab hold of anything tangible resembling her. I rack my brain to the point of a headache after almost picking up the phone to call and say hello. "Why doesn't the number go to her anymore? What happened to our direct line?" Then, when I have momentarily calmed down, I think about how comforting a hug from her would be, and the cycle starts over. I am not a grown man. I am still a child that pulls at her arm and nags, hoping to be held; a child still begging for care and nurturing. I need the tenderness of her existence that is imbedded in the womb and forever protected by the bonds of birth.

It was then instilled in both of us that she is to be recognized as my physical creator. She, and she alone, holds the key which has access to these comforting qualities.

In my eyes, God could not provide the palpable concreteness I needed to plug the gaps of my broken heart. To be perfectly honest, I had not asked either. That night, as a snowstorm blanketed the rest of Texas, I found God in a Wal-Mart parking lot while searching for warmth in the backseat of my vehicle. The rest of my time down by the coast, I felt like someone was with me. When I was in the water surfing (yes, I still went in the water), when I was watching the sun rise on the shoreline, and while I sat next to my bonfire on the beach drinking His holy wine under the stars, I had an undeniable sense I was not alone; all because I had finally asked. The feeling was wonderful.

The accompaniment did not last long, and the loneliness did not dissipate in the matter of a few days. There was still much to be done. As I opened the front door to our apartment, I peered up the stairs, dreading being back. I didn't even make it halfway up the steps before collapsing, having to bury my face in my hands out of shame for how much I had come to hate my life. It was a make-or-break moment, and I decided I couldn't consistently take it one more day. Each morning I rose early to a scriptural devotional. I then spent an hour working out, followed by lunch, and one more thing that gave me joy. I had to force myself out of bed. I had to force myself to leave the house in search of an undiscovered park or creek to explore. I explored nature, and I explored in search of answers to some of life's most challenging questions. Every Thursday evening before my small group I had dinner with my Aunt Junie. She gave me short, fleeting glimpses of my mother, and those glimpses began to set me at ease. This is how the digging process began.

What I unearthed was how people are just smart enough to run themselves silly in circles in search of answers. Despite all of the technological advances and societal progressions we like to take so much credit for, we have an enormous amount of difficulty seeing past the small confines of tragedy. As humans, we're hardwired to desire answers for everything! We want to know for sure something is true in order to place it in the category of a fact; something indisputable. These facts act as warm blankets to our previous premises until the next scientific breakthrough occurs, dispelling old notions and instilling new facts in their place. But what does this say to us? It says what many other scientists are saying; that speculatively, approximately 80 percent of the earth's secrets have yet to be uncovered.

We want answers. We demand answers. We lose sight of the bigger picture, not willing to accept anything except an answer to many questions that are simply unanswerable. People often ask, "Why me? Why her? Why do bad things happen to good people?" What I want to know is: how have these become some of the more frequently asked questions, which demand answers that don't always exist in understandable forms to our longing minds? Instead, the quick fix is to turn to a pill, or to start blaming people. We blame doctors. We blame other friends and family members in the midst of misfortune. Worst, God becomes the greatest target of our blame. Then the questions turn to issues of justice. "Why didn't He stop this? Why does He let us suffer? Why weren't our prayers *answered*?" Oh, how quickly we forget the hardships of important figures in the Bible, and how they still maintained their faith by refusing to blame God.

We are so quick to forget the trials of Job. Job was the wealthiest and most faithful man to God in all of his area. Unannounced to him, he was being tested by the enemy to assess the strength of his devotion. He lost all of his finances, followed by all of his children, but still praised God, even in the wake of his devastation. He was then stricken with a terrible case of boils. Alone, poor, and diseased, he finally became bitter in his questioning of God's supposed curse on his life. It wasn't until Job acknowledged that he could never understand the depths of God's will that his faith was restored in Him. Immediately after, God returned everything to Job that had been taken from him twofold.

We are so quick to forget about Paul and Silas being beaten and thrown in jail for performing one of God's acts. Imprisoned, they sang and praised His name until an earthquake shook the shackles off their feet, the stocks off their arms, and blew the dungeons doors wide open for them to go free. However, they didn't leave until they had saved the guard from taking his own life in fear of the miracle he had just seen, and they saved his life eternally by leading him to the Lord before being pardoned.

We are so quick to forget that Daniel, Shadrach, Meshach, and Abednego were taken from their fallen lands of Jerusalem and made to be servants for the new king. In their time they never once stopped serving God. Every chance they got, they were used to disprove sorcery and magic; finding favor in a foreign king's eyes. These were the same men that walked unscathed in a fiery furnace and were saved from the lion's den for refusing to praise any deity other than the Almighty.

We are so quick to forget about Joseph in the book of Genesis. Joseph was despised by all of his older brothers for their father's favoritism toward him when he gave Joseph a coat of many colors. They were enraged by the dreams that Joseph had depicting they would all bow to their youngest brother one day. He was sold into slavery by his own brothers, and then the gift of his father was used to lie about his death when they painted the coat with the blood of a goat they killed. He was bought by the captain of the palace guard, finding favor with him. He was then entrusted with his master's entire household, only to be put in prison when his master's wife falsely claimed rape out of anger after he refused to sleep with her. After years in prison he helped a man get out by interpreting his dream, only asking that the man remember him later. He was forgotten about for another two years, but found favor with the jailer and was put in charge of all the prisoners. Joseph's faith never gave way, and each time something terrible happened to him scriptures read, "The Lord was with Joseph." Three times the Bible specifically says the Lord was with him. Twice more it says his masters' recognized the Lord was with him also.

Later he was freed and promoted to the head of all Egypt, second only to the command of Pharaoh, for interpreting a dream proclaiming seven years of prosperity and seven years of famine. During his post, two beautiful things happened. First, in Genesis 41:52, he named one of his sons Ephraim; Hebrew for, "fruitful" and said, "God has made me fruitful in this land of my *suffering*." Second, during the famine, after Joseph had the foresight to store a fifth of all the goods from the seven years of prosperity, Joseph's brothers unknowingly came to him and bowed down, starving for food. He finally unveiled himself in Genesis 45:4–5 saying, "I am Joseph, your brother whom you sold into Egypt. But don't be angry with yourselves that you did this to me, for

God did it. He sent me here ahead of you to preserve your lives."

Dwell on the power of those two verses. Despite slavery, false rape accusations, and prison; all beginning with his brothers' betrayal, he gives praise to God for the end result of a plan that he could not see at the time. Not only that, but he *forgives* his brothers, and says he endured all of this to give them *life*! Had he blamed God and wasted too much time asking for answers, his faith would not have been as strong as it needed to be to find favor with God. Without God's favor, he would have never found favor with his masters. Without their favor he could have never found it in his heart to forgive. And without his forgiveness his brothers' lives could not have been saved. His forgiveness gave his entire family *life*, and it all goes back to his faith in the Lord no matter the circumstances.

These stories lead me to two frightening issues of our day. Somewhere at some point, people got together and devised a master marketing plan. It took a while to perfect; it was created with quiet investments and multiple small sales all over the country, but today it is a finely tuned machine. Their trials were successful. These people now efficiently sell us the false product of entitlement—it's all around us. They are the ones on television saying, "Because you're beautiful," "because you're worth it," "because you deserve it." If it's not in the advertisements, it's in the programs. Images of materialism and unobtainable amounts of wealth and beauty are portrayed as to be the lifestyles everyone should be enjoying. The problem with all of this is that it creates the sense we are all *entitled* to rewards that don't equate with efforts. Our society has difficulty distinguishing that reality TV is not reality, but in fact another well marketed form of entertainment. Therefore, we lose sight of all the evidence telling us a well proven concept within the *reality* of life: we don't deserve anything we have not diligently worked toward, and things will not simply be handed to us.

It would seem that this is common knowledge, but the idea actually runs contrary to the quick-fix sentiments that advertisers and the media have constructed. A single pill is promoted to be the solution for any ailment one might ever have, and we demand instantaneous results; instantaneous answers. Life was never set up to work this way, and that is why there will always be side effects to the quick fix. When we don't get the results we were looking for, within the time frame we desire, apathy sets in. "Well," we think, "things didn't go the way they were supposed to, so this must be a punishment. This must be somebody else's fault. There must be somebody else to blame."

Our reliance on someone else to handle our problems for us has ultimately given way to a lack of faith, and lack of faith gives way to fear. It appears on every single news channel there is fear blasting from the mouths of every reporter. We are made to believe there is a terrorist lurking underneath each of our beds. We are inundated with the fear of our delicate economy, of losing our jobs, our healthcare, and our homes. Oh, "In these times ..." they say. Well, what do we really have to fear in this country? Have you noticed the runners scrolling quickly along the bottom of your television screen? Many of them detail civilian casualties of war taking place in the streets of faraway countries, or deaths from roadside bombs going off every day. It seems pathetic to me that we don't take the time to appreciate the peacefulness of living in the United States. Yet, we all fall into the trap that we are supposed to be afraid.

In these times this ... and in these times that. "In these times," has become the preface of every excuse existing today for contributions the majority of our society is no longer willing to put in towards long-lasting solutions. I am sick of "our times." If we trusted God, we would know He is our provider, and our diligence to His word will reap the benefits of all of our needs. If we truly trusted God we would praise him for being able to comfortably stroll down any sidewalk without fear of the parked cars exploding, or of a rebel military force suddenly opening fire in our markets or yards. The tales of Joseph, Paul, and Daniel are not just fun tales from our Bible school days as children. They are powerful promises by God, showing He will not forsake us when we put our trust in Him. It is said in the Bible that we were created in His image, and given the freedom of choice. We are not puppets, and we must also accept shared responsibility for our actions. Yes, He wants to answer your prayers, but He has to see the sincerity of your heart first. Life is not a game. It is a test; a test of our endurance, our integrity in adverse situations, and our faith in Him.

In photography, when trying to calculate lighting in your shot, to find the source of light one must first find the darkest point. Within that pocket of darkness, light is a form of energy moving in to fill the gap, thus revealing itself. The term for this is "motivated light." I'm inspired by this idea—not only is light trying to fill every dark crevasse, but it is also *naturally motivated* to do so. This is a fitting analogy. Once God's light is finally able to shine on your darkest moments, you will be energized and *motivated* to step out into its full glorified shine.

When I became rejuvenated by a newly motivated mind-set, I began to dwell on my mother's life. Years before, when she was on her own trying to make ends meet; she would clean homes and cut hair on the side. It seemed unglamorous to reflect on us living in a day-care center; I equated it with some sort of halfway-house assistance. I remember asking her how hard it must have been for her back then. She said, "Are you kidding me? The day-care gig was a dream come true. The only thing I wanted to do was spend time with my baby. I couldn't imagine leaving you in someone else's hands and missing out on all of those precious moments each day while I went out to work. There, it was my job to play with children, which included my own. I got to spend every second with you!" Her perception of every situation was always such a gut check. Her cup was never half-empty, or even just full. Her cup was always overflowing.

I began to ask questions in a completely different form. Yes, she was too young (by my standards) to be gone, and I still needed her in my life, but she'd been able to accomplish in less time what most people refuse to do with more. What can I do to make the most out of what she has taught me? How can God still use her life to make others' and mine better? What was the purpose of her existence? How can I be an extension of her, to reach out to those in need?

It goes as follows:

While there is still so much left unanswered for me, I have enough to work with now to strive toward peace in my heart. Her greatest longing for living was to serve God by helping others. I don't know why His plan is more effective with her in heaven. Maybe we have become desensitized and disenchanted with fairy-tale endings. Maybe deep down, our society is sick of superficialities and ready for the honesty of the reality that death is a part of life, and not everyone survives living happily ever after on earth. If her life has the potential to touch exponentially more lives this way, then so be it.

Through her lessons, I have learned to embrace the suffering for its ability to humble me back to a place that forced a necessary re-evaluation of my life and my values. No longer do I put my faith and confidence in the things I've done. Now my life is devoted to the Lord, a commitment that losing her taught me to make on my own. I now know how to seek Him and praise Him for what I do have, and what I was blessed to have had.

These are times of absolutes. I was at my absolute lowest. Now I am absolutely grateful for the person my mother was. She earned my suffering. She was the absolute greatest mother I could have ever asked for, and she deserves my loving tears. Her place in our hearts is emboldened by our mourning, and I will no longer run from her memory. She taught me how to love others well. She taught me grace and the life of forgiveness. She taught me the definition of absolute, unwavering strength. She taught me the integrity of faith and prayer, and how they are everyday necessities to achieve favor in God's eyes. Without diligence in our faith and prayer, we will give up and fail. She taught me not accept either.

She taught me the true essence of one's legacy; the impact one has on the lives of others. She taught me to be fierce and mighty in the face of adversity. She taught me how to be obedient to the Lord's plan for my life, even when I cannot see what is around the corner.

This is a story of life, even in death, because she continues to teach me every day. This is what makes her so inspiring; her life was a rare gift I wish to give back to the world. She overlooked one thing in her time spent with us though. She was diligent to her work here. As a person and as a parent there is nothing better you can do for your children than to love them and to live diligently to your work on earth. A child's mind is like a sponge; it will soak up everything around it, and a child will believe he can do anything he is encouraged to achieve. At some point though, someone will tell him that he is incapable of making his dreams a reality. Fortunately, my mommy got to my dreams before anyone else. She told me she is real and could see all of my greatest accomplishments! She *is* real; she still exists in heaven, and was diligent in her work here. She raised a grateful and loving son, and I have told her story. For that, God can effectively use her life, even from the grave.

For those who are still stuck on the wrong questions, and want to know if my mother's prayers were answered; well, if you've made it this far, what's to say they haven't been already…

Acknowledgements

THIS BOOK WAS written with a heavy heart and an equal amount of joy. Its conception and fruition would have never been possible without the love and support of my family and friends. I give those closest to me shared credit for this achievement. They kept me motivated, offered ceaseless assistance and showed me more patience and grace than I feel I deserved at times. While this tale mostly documented a personal journey through my mother's battles, Anna touched the lives of so many others around her. I apologize that there is not enough space for everyone to illustrate their hearts for my mom. However, I would have considered it an injustice not to include the voices of the people who shared many of the same special moments that I was fortunate to have had with her. It is a blessing and an honor to leave you in the company of their loving testimonies now. Thank you so much to everyone who made God from the Grave possible.

Testimonies

On a crisp, seemingly uneventful day in January 1992, I sat with my dearest friend Anna in her kitchen. It was in Austin, Texas. John was at work, Tyler in school, and Hilary napping. When your hearts are knitted so closely together, as ours were, even the mundane things were special. She was that friend who, even when we went for long periods without seeing each other, made the moment we reunited feel instantly like we had never been apart; like sisters.

We had met at Band Camp in early summer 1977. We were about to enter our 7th grade year at Peterson Junior High in Kerrville, Texas. Anna was the funniest girl I had ever met. Everyone loved being around her. Her joy and zeal for life was contagious, never a dull moment. From that time I learned that she had a wonderful family whom I grew to love as well. Through the years, we grew together and even when we grew apart, we still shared the greatest bond of all…Christ. It was Anna who demanded my attention return to my first love during college, the Lord. She didn't give up when I turned my back on her requests to attend her wonderful church. I am so thankful for her "in your face" boldness.

On that January day I went into labor with my first child. She took charge, as always was her nature. She got me to the hospital and spent the next few days helping me through the new realities of motherhood. I would have to say that through all of the years, and all of the wonderful times, Anna's greatest expression of joy was her family. She taught me this. From that day of giving birth to my daughter until she stepped into heaven, the example she set has given me vision to cherish my family. I always saw her put family first. John, her children, and all of her family were the most dear to her. Anna's legacy will challenge me all the days of my life to strive to put my own pursuits aside so that I too can leave that heritage to my children, who were all blessed to know her as well.

-Sandra Adkins

Whenever I don't feel well, and I am tempted not to follow through on a commitment, I automatically think of Anna. I picked her up for church every

Sunday at 10:20am. Sometimes she needed help dressing. Every time, she needed help getting into the car. One Sunday, we actually had to pull over to the side and let her throw up. She then smiled and said, "Aw. I feel fine now."

It hurt her to sit in the wheelchair for long periods, but she refused to let the enemy prevent her from going to church. At the end of service, she wanted us to hurry and take her out, but that never happened. My husband would push her toward the door, and without fail someone always needed to say something to her, prayer or counsel. She would always say softly, "Please stop," and J.L. would come to a sudden halt.

One day I watched her from my dining room window walking up my sidewalk. I felt like she should have been at home lying down, but she had been up fulfilling a commitment to decorate for one of her daughter's, Hilary, senior projects. As she made her way to my door, she dragged her feet and took deep, long breaths. I wondered why she was using her energy to come to my house. It was my birthday, she explained, and she had a present for me.

When I am tired, weak, or just not feeling well, I shake myself and say, "Get over this. It's nothing compared to what Anna endured." And it's true. No one compares to Anna Rambeau. She was just "all that."

-Linda Crawford

Anna was such a strong and brave person and I admired her very much.

She gave her testimony during the first Women's Meeting we had, and it was an eye opener for me. Anna said, God sees your hurting heart and your empty arms, and He loves you.

It was my story she was telling, except the part where she was allowed to keep her baby. Anna said that we are loved by God no matter what we have done and He will never leave you. You are His child and He forgives us if we ask, and we have to forgive our self.

I was so full of shame and here she was so free to tell her story. After hearing her that night I have been able to talk about my life, and was able to forgive myself from some things in the past. Anna left a mark in my heart for a deeper walk with God, and touched my life in a way that I will carry with me always.

-Julia Rodgers

Several years ago, during one of the healing services in the big sanctuary, I heard God softly calling "Anna, Anna." I remember thinking, "Why am I hearing God call Anna's name?" Immediately a word came to me that I shared with her afterward. Here it is: Anna was the name of Mary's mother, and just as she raised up someone so precious to God that He chose her to be the mother of his son, Jesus, Anna was also raising up someone or something that was (is) very precious to God, and will touch many lives.

That was it; short, sweet and powerful! Maybe it is one of her children, or the wonderful ministry she had. Maybe it is this book; honoring her legacy that will reach more people than we can imagine for our sweet- Jesus. There is no doubt in my mind that something wonderful is coming from Anna's life. I remember and think of her often with much love and thankfulness for many reasons, but just wanted to share this word for encourage and blessings.

-Donna Dyer

I had just lost my husband of thirty-three years. Anna was very attentive to me. Even in exercise class she would constantly look back (she was in front of the class) and mouth to me, "Are you ok?" Usually I would give her thumbs up, but there were times when I would just crumble to the floor. Anna would hold me, rock me in her arms, and comfort me, all the while praying for me, while both of us would be crying. Then one day, about eighteen months after his passing, she told me to come to her office after class. We met, and of course I was a blubbering mess.

She sat me down, held me and prayed with me. I looked into those brown eyes of hers and saw so much love and compassion. She said she loved me, and was here for whatever I needed, then took my face in her hands and said with such care, "Butch is dead. He is in heaven, and does not want to come back here. Why would he? He is walking, not paralyzed anymore. He is whole and healed." In that moment I realized I was being selfish and wanted him to come back to me. Even though I had been grieving all of those months, that day my healing began and I owe it all to my loving pastor, Anna.

I truly feel, had she not been sensitive to the Holy Spirit, my grieving would have turned into an eternal captivity. Some would think that would have been harsh, but I am forever grateful for her boldness. Anna I love you and miss you. I am thankful you are not in my past, but in my future. I know you are decorating on, so go girl. I love you sister.

-Debbie Harvey

To my sweet Anna: it was not who she was to me, but who she was not that changed me the most.

She was NOT ever selfish. She was about others. She dropped everything on a regular basis to help people decorate or even clean. She even got a baby sitter for her own children to drive to Colorado and help us move, which I said I didn't need help with, but could not have done without her and John.

She was NOT ever negative. Every time I hung up the phone with her, my heart was encouraged. Whether we were talking about losing weight, raising children, our husbands, or even cancer, her hope was contagious. I echo the words of her daughter who said, "She made this so easy on us!" when referring to Anna's fight with cancer; that says it all.

She was NOT ever faithless. I have never met anyone who so readily applied prayer and scripture to every situation. She believed in and expected God to move in every situation. Even when her body was the weakest, her priority was to get that CD player pumping out the Word!

Mark and I miss our friend, and my kids miss their Aunt, but Anna's influence in all of our lives is eternal. To Anna, her life was not about this life but about the one she is living now. I am so grateful to have been a direct beneficiary of the eternal fruit produced in her life.

-Aunt Jenny (Snelling)

I named her Anna Rambeautiful because she was such a beauty to me, a true princess and reflection of the King. She brought all of her life before her God as if He was right next to her all the time, inviting His assistance in *everything.* Anna never judged me, but would challenge me with Kingdom principles on my thoughts and decisions, that would ultimately bring me freedom and peace.

She loved bringing joy to another's heart. She still holds the standard for me to this day because I continue to ask myself, "How would Anna do this or handle that?" She also modeled such a true "mother's heart" in the way she loved her kiddos. It was a beautiful thing to witness the love she had for her husband as well, honoring and serving him.

Speaking life into every situation was just her way. Anna approached everything with a "can do" attitude, always so positive no matter what the situation. "If you say it's going be hard, it will be. Speak things that are not as though they are." That girl just made it seem like we could do anything!

With her I could be myself. She was a kind and safe place. We tried all kinds of painting techniques, watched Creflo in the mornings, and then called each other singing "I'm a world changer." We would read the map over the phone to each other when traveling alone so we didn't get lost, and to keep each other company.

We had a heart connection like I have never known in a friend. When she left us, I struggled to put in words what she meant to me. The Spirit woke me just after retiring for bed the night before the funeral with these words…

"The song of your life had a melody like no other and I am made better having heard the music".

-Julie Wilson

When we moved to Waco ten years ago we were immediately drawn to John and Anna, and sought guidance from them for many of life's natural challenges. It was nice to see how Anna's advice always worked, because she lived what she preached. I admired her, cherished our friendship and the example she provided as a wife and mother.

A few years ago, Greg got a convertible "date car" and we formed the Top-Down small group with John and Anna. Occasionally we'd meet for lunch or breakfast while the kids were at school, then cruise around in our convertibles. Even during her journey with cancer, she managed to enjoy this, and even joked about how she no longer had to worry about her hair flying in her face during our rides. I cared for many people battling cancer while working for ten years as an oncology nurse, many of whom were believers, but not until Anna had I ever known someone who lived, breathed, and spoke the *truth* in *all* things! I learned so much from her, but hoped I'd never have to apply her teachings to similar hardships. However, the day following her funeral, my dad was diagnosed with terminal brain cancer. Over the next five months, I learned just how hard it is to live that truth day in and day out. It was a daily decision, and yet, she made it look so easy in all things! My respect for her is continually growing.

I had the opportunity to work with her on several projects at our children's school, before she left to dance in heaven. I loved how she had a way of asking you to help with something without ever allowing the chance for you to say no! I wish I'd learned that skill from her so I could use it at home with the kids, but I always enjoyed our time together. She never asked anything that she was not also willing to do. She truly gave us her all.

-Amanda Newman

I am nine years older than Anna, my sister, and I can still remember the day she was born like it was yesterday. I grew up thinking of Anna as my own child, a sister, and best friend. In 2008 I had the opportunity to escort Anna to a small Texas court house to testify on behalf of a terrible car accident she had witnessed, in which a young woman unnecessarily lost her life.

Anna was going through chemotherapy then, and was thin and bald, but we still had fun making a fuss over her cute outfit and the hat she was wearing.

I have spent a considerable amount of time in courts because of my job, and had this overwhelming sense of feeling the need to protect her from many of the games I've seen played, but it was she who ended up protecting all of us there that day. The trial was settled out of court that morning and her testimony was no longer necessary. I watched as Anna brought the girl's surviving family members together to answer questions they had longed to know for over a year. The details were painful to hear, but the peace of God was in the room as she delivered a powerful message to each of them. I admired her seemingly angelic delivery.

I saw this small woman become an ambassador for Jesus. Her words and actions brought comfort where none seemed possible. Driving home I marveled at how her physical body did not appear mighty, but her faith in God being with us all was enormous. Not one of us left the court house the same that day because of my youngest sister.

-Aunt Junie (Plummer)

While my sisters and I have accumulated many fond memories together, I would like to tell you how well my sister could put a gathering together. When our brother, Bill, passed away it was a very cold day. We needed to write an obituary, make funeral arrangements, contact friends, and our local newspaper in Kerrville where we grew up. Anna was at the forefront of all of these.

It was a difficult time for our family that left many of us unable to respond appropriately within the allotted time. Despite her being the youngest sibling, Anna's strength always shown through as an absolute blessing when we needed her most. In three days she put together a video with Bill's baby pictures, arranged for flowers to be delivered to the front alter of the church, picked out music, and arranged a luncheon afterwards with all of his friends in attendance. Even the cards she had printed, with a fitting poem on the back, had all of Anna's personal touches that made her so special. Somehow, even in sadness, she managed to turn Bill's funeral into a joyous celebration. It was the perfect and befitting tribute to her love and compassion for our brother.

-Aunt Christine (Taylor)

I can't say that I personally knew Anna Rambeau, but I greatly admired her. She knew exactly who she was, and this was proven when John became our pastor. She put a new face on what we perceived was a pastor's wife. It was evident that she helped her husband in every way she could.

She also put a new face on the building interior of the church. She turned the building into a beautiful place. The bathrooms were no longer just functional, they were gorgeous. She upgraded every entrance that I came through with paint, plants, and beautiful furniture. I'm just sorry that I never told her how much I appreciated her efforts to make the building so beautiful.

-Mercile Duggan

Anna was an angel to me. She always had a hug and a big bright smile that made you feel like you had just embraced an angel. She and Pastor John have prayed for me a number of times, and the spirit of her conviction was so strong and sincere. It just made my day to see her. This was a lady that lived her life totally for the glory and honor of her Savior!

I feel very honored and Blessed to have known her.

-Janis Bell

PUMA

About the Family

John Rambeau (Dad)

John is the pastor of a local church in Waco, Texas, where he continues to raise the children who are left under his roof. Along with a true servant's heart, the consistency of his integrity has helped him find favor in everything he has ever set his mind to, and shown as a guiding light to all who know him. With an admirable blend of character traits, he is the epitome of what every man should aspire to be. He is the rock and provider of his family, steady in his authority and forever forgiving, diligent to his work, but has never neglected his number one priority at home (family). He has a kind heart that welcomes all with open arms, and stands as a beacon of excellence in all that he does.

Hilary Rambeau

Hilary is a gorgeous young woman, and attends the University of Arkansas, where she has excelled in her academic and extracurricular activities alike. She has the warmest and whackiest personality out of anyone you'll ever meet. There is pure joy in her aura, and a bit of God's healing exists in her laughter that is felt often. She quickly found a calling for the ministry in mission work after volunteering in Thailand and working as a counselor at Camp Kanakuk this past summer. Hilary has plans to continue serving in less fortunate countries every chance she gets.

Christian Rambeau

Christian is tall and handsome like his father. He is an incredibly gifted musician, but has recently focused his devotion to his love for basketball; fitting being that he is passionate and driven by the success of his hard work ethic. While attending high school, he is recognized for his humorous antics by both friends and teachers. People naturally gravitate to his charisma, but when he isn't busy cracking jokes he has the ability to speak with intelligence well beyond his years. Still youthful in a stage of searching and maturing, he contains all of the equipment to ripen into a wonderful man who will know exactly who he is in the Lord and live accordingly.

Rachel Rambeau

Rachel is the youngest and sweetest of the bunch. She bears striking resemblances to her mother in appearance and demeanor. She has the same beautiful little face, brown hair and eyes to match, as Anna. With a celestial smile, she also has a spirit of compassion and an identical love for animals and her family. She speaks softly and there is innocence in everything she does. She contains brilliant creativity as well; attracting many followers to the fun things she conjures up. When Rachel decided she no longer liked the context of the word "bye," she instead began saying, "Hi Hi," to let you know you will see her again soon, as well as saying, "Love Love," to reinforce how much she appreciated our mother. Her lingo caught on with every kid in class.

Hi hi and love love to all of you.

CPSIA information can be obtained at www.ICGtesting.com
229002LV00007B/40/P

9 781456 321963